CONFLICT RESOLUTION

A Blueprint for Preventing School Violence

Mary Meggie

Steven W. Edwards

Kenneth Gwozdz

EAST HARTFORD HIGH SCHOOL, CONNECTICUT

NEW YORK
THE SOLOMON PRESS, PUBLISHERS

Conflict Resolution: A Blueprint for Preventing School Violence

by Mary Meggie, Steven W. Edwards, and Kenneth Gwozdz

The Solomon Press
        98-12 66th Avenue, Suite #2
        Rego Park, NY 11374 USA
        phone: 718-830-9112
        fax: 718-830-0351
        email: solomon@dialfree.ws

        This book was designed by Sidney Solomon
        and typeset by Eve Brant in Galliard, Quorum, and Eras fonts

First printing June, 2001   ISBN: 0-934623-74-0

Contents

Two Forewords   vii
    DR. GERALD N. TIROZZI, Executive Director,
        National Association of Secondary School
        Principals
    JOAN BARALOTO, Director of Education and
        Family Initiatives, Community Relations,
        USA Today

Introduction   1

Chapter 1   5
    Rationale:
        Why Every Community Needs a
        Student Assistance Center

Chapter 2   18
    Start Up: Beginnings Are Not Easy

Chapter 3   29
    Mediations: Empowering Students

Chapter 4   39
    Sample SAC Mediations and Student Interviews

Chapter 5   69
    Other Elements of the SAC:
        How to Make Your Program Fit
        Your Community

Chapter 6   75
    Support Services and Agencies

Chapter 7   83
    Winning Your Public

Chapter 8   89
    Funding

Chapter 9   93
    The SAC's Success

Conclusion   97

Appendices
    1. Timeline   101
    2. SAC Needs-Assessment Survey   102
    3. SAC Set-Up–Architectural Design/Logistics   104
    4. Help Shape the Future–Career Beginnings   105
    5. Mediation Agreement Form   106
    6. Peer Mediation Application   107
    7. Overview of SAT Procedures   108
    8. SAC Referral Form   109
    9. Behaviors of Concern Form   110
    10. SAC Intake Form   111
    11. SAC Reply Form   112
    12. Confidential Alert List (Sample)   113
    13. Drug and Alcohol Insight Group   114
    14. Substance Abuse Survey   115
    15. Student Interest Questionnaire   116

Selected Bibliography   118

East Hartford High School   120
    Student Assistance Center Awards

Two Forewords

With prevention first and consequences second, East Hartford High School staff have developed a model for conflict prevention and resolution that is easily replicable for all schools committed to proactive, student-centered strategies. The vehicle is a Student Assistance Center. After only one year in existence, the school reported a 44 percent reduction in suspensions and detentions. This impressive outcome requires examination. *Conflict Resolution: A Blueprint for Preventing School Violence* is a welcome document to the canon of literature available for keeping schools safe, nurturing havens for all students.

Schools need the assistance and support of parents, social services agencies, and governmental and business partners to meet the increasing needs of students. This manual provides a comprehensive strategy for enlisting and partnering with key stakeholders, and describes services that should be available in a student assistance center.

As a nationally recognized program, I salute and applaud the Student Assistance Center at East Hartford High School for sharing their strategy that works! I am confident that you will find much food for thought in this handbook, as well as tools to use in your own school community. —Dr. Gerald N. Tirozzi

Executive Director

National Association of Secondary School Principals

Dr. Tirozzi served as Connecticut's Educational Commissioner in the 1980s before becoming an Assistant U. S. Secretary of Education under President Clinton.

"Outstanding. Exciting. Clearly a cutting-edge, effective program." These were among the comments from judges—leading educators—when they read about East Hartford High School's

Student Assistance Center. After I spent time with the school's students, faculty, and administrators, I knew our judges were right.

USA Today, in its continuing commitment to education, had announced in 1993 a national recognition program that identified outstanding grass-roots programs which improved learning opportunities for young people through comprehensive community involvement. The winning programs were featured in a publication, *Community Solutions for Education*, supported by USA Today, Apple Computer, Procter & Gamble's Crest and Tide brands, Sallie Mae, State Farm Insurance, and Subaru of America.

In 1995, thousands of committees applied for the recognition program, but there were only seven national winners. The judges overwhelmingly voted the Student Assistance Center at East Hartford High School one of those winners. The program clearly fulfilled the Community Solutions for Education criteria:

√ United the community in support of education to meet a critical need
√ Encouraged the sustained cooperation of the community
√ Showed tangible evidence of success
√ Demonstrated effective use of resources
√ Served as a model for other communities

One of the recognition program's requirements was that winners had to be willing to help other communities replicate their success. It was that requirement which led to this book. The East Hartford High School staff has unselfishly assisted over 1,000 districts across the United States plan and implement their own Student Assistance Centers. More than 350 institutions physically visited East Hartford High School.

The unmistakable evidence of the program's worth has been its continued growth and success. That's a testimonial to the school's leadership and spirit.

It is regretable that our society is awash with so many problems, but the solutions lie in creative, positive programs like East Hartford's Student Assistance Center.   —Joan Baraloto
Director of Education and Family Initiatives
USA TODAY

Introduction

A Snapshot of School Violence in the News

♦ March 7, 2001—One wounded in Williamsport, PA, by a 14-year-old girl

♦ March 5, 2001—Two killed and 13 wounded in Santee, CA

♦ February 29, 2000—One six-year-old shot and killed by a classmate

♦ December 6, 1999—Four wounded at Fort Gibson Middle School in Fort Gibson, OK

♦ May 20, 1999—Six wounded in Conyers, GA

♦ April 20, 1999—15 dead and 23 wounded in Littleton, CO

♦ April 16, 1999—Sophomore fires two shotgun blasts in a school hallway in Notus, ID—no one is injured

♦ June 15, 1998—Two wounded in Richmond, VA

♦ May 21, 1998—Two teenagers fatally shot and twenty-two injured in Springfield, OR

♦ May 19, 1998—One dead in Fayetteville, TN

♦ April 24, 1998—One dead and one wounded in Edinboro, PA

♦ March 24, 1998—Five dead and 10 wounded in Jonesboro, AR

♦ December 15, 1997—Two wounded in Stamps, AR

♦ December 1, 1997—Three dead and five wounded in West Paducah, KY

♦ October 1, 1997—Two dead and seven wounded in Pearl, MS

If these tragic incidents and 19 deaths in public schools between October, 1997, and April 16, 1999, did not put educators on notice, the 15 deaths that followed in laid-back Littleton, Colorado, did. As the suburban tragedy of affluent Columbine High School

1

will attest, no community and no school is immune to violence. That unprecedented shooting rampage by two teens with semiautomatic weapons and a homemade arsenal of explosives should serve as a tragic wake-up call to all educators: Crises like this can happen anywhere.

We are cautioned not to look for a pattern. "Is it the absence of parents, the presence of guns, the cruelty of the culture, the culture of cruelty?" queried one reporter after the Santana High School tragedy (Gibbs, 22).

Recent violent incidents have prompted a peek under the curtain of silence about violence in our schools. Officials at schools around the country have long known of violent school extortionists, weapon use, firebombing, sexual assaults, and staff and student beatings. With increasing media attention, the problem of school violence now becomes shared among families and educators, nationally and around the world.

In April, 1999, one student was killed and another was wounded in Taber, Alberta, Canada, when a fourteen-year-old opened fire. Now come reports that as notoriously proud and generally peaceful France struggles with chronic unemployment and cultural unrest, "a plague of school violence" has been stealing across that country in the past decade ("Violence...," A3).

No one is immune. Communities can no longer live with their heads in the sand. Nor can they afford to hide their problems from public scrutiny. Violence in our schools is undeniably one of the most challenging issues facing educators today. Safety must become a priority. The issue assumed national prominence when then-President Bush and the nation's 50 governors declared in the National Education Goals 2000 that all schools need to be drug free and violence free as well as maintain an environment that is both disciplined and conducive to learning (Caudle, 1994).

In proactive responses to escalating problems of the early 1990s, many educators instituted get-tough policies and a no-tolerance attitude toward use of drugs, alcohol, weapons, or acts of violence. These strict disciplinary measures are considered necessary for the safety and well being of the general student body, as well as faculty and staff.

But alone, these measures are not enough. By 1992, with the steady increase in acts of violence, gangs, weapons, drug activity, and other antisocial behaviors in schools, suspensions and expulsions were skyrocketing. In addition to having a strict code of conduct, districts *must also* establish proactive programs to provide students with positive alternatives for conflict resolution. While a number of programs were already in place in various schools, they needed to be consolidated, fine-tuned, and coordinated to better serve the student population.

At East Hartford High School in East Hartford, Connecticut, a Student Assistance Center (SAC) that would become a national model was taking shape.

A ZERO-tolerance policy for drugs and violence was put in place at the outset, backed by strict rules and regulations and comprehensive Board of Education policy. In tackling school violence, the SAC's founders looked at prevention first and consequences second. Conflict prevention and resolution were the goals and peer mediation the main tool, with student mediators being given formal training in the mediation process. Despite a tight school budget, a director was assigned to the SAC. Teachers and other staff were invited to participate, both in running the SAC and in identifying and referring students who could benefit from it.

As East Hartford's SAC gained momentum and credibility, requests to share the model with other educators began to pour in. Students were empowered by their role as mediators, while disputants felt increasingly responsible for resolving their own problems. Teachers and the community saw the effectiveness of the SAC. The Center expanded, evolved, and changed with its students' needs, adding Alcoholics Anonymous, Narcotics Anonymous, a domestic violence prevention program, and other group's meeting on site.

Today, East Hartford High School's SAC is a vibrant and integral part of the school, conducting mediations, reaching out to students referred by teachers and other staff, and providing kids with a safe place to go when they need help. It is making one-to-one connections and making a difference for the many, many students who would otherwise fall through the cracks.

Equally important, it empowers students with the tools and the skills they need to resolve disputes themselves before they become violent.

The components of the SAC can be easily replicated and incorporated seamlessly into any school or institution to help create a safe, vibrant school environment. Here's how.

Chapter 1

Rationale
*Why Every Community Needs
a Student Assistance Center*

The Educator's Role and Responsibility
Bullying: Mean-Free Classrooms
Assertive Parenting
What Can Administrators Do?
East Hartford High School and the Student Assistance Center

5

T here is a whole new category of kids out there who emanate from dysfunctional families. I call it the "Urban Orphan." They might be involved in a family, but the family is so dysfunctional that they go to school and unload in the classroom. These problems are non-academic and totally outside the curriculum. (Brady, 1996)

In 1990, then-President George Bush and the governors of all 50 states established National Education Goals, targeting the year 2000 to achieve them. These eight goals, covering myriad topics, were selected because political and educational leaders alike were convinced that they were critical to the success of public education. Goal Number 7 states that:

> By the year 2000, every school in the United States will be free of drugs, violence, and the unauthorized presence of firearms and alcohol and will offer a disciplined environment conducive to learning. (National Education Goals Panel, 1995)

The mere fact that school safety has been elevated to one of these eight objectives nationally speaks to the significance of this threat and the public's demand for safe schools.

More than three million crimes a year are committed in or near our public schools (Toch et al., 1993). While the public may support higher educational standards, it seriously questions whether they can be achieved when schools are confronted with safety concerns daily ("A Place for Every Youth...," 1995). Safety is even more difficult to address considering the burgeoning role our schools have been forced to assume—particularly that of surrogate family. Kenneth Burnley, Superintendent of Schools in Colorado Springs, Colorado, voices this concern:

> Schools have become mom, dad, church and community. It's a Catch-22. We're at the point where before we can educate kids, we have to peel off the problems from the night before. (Stratton, 1995)

To teach children, schools must first be able to reach them. Our schools are feeling the repercussions of the increasing severity of problems facing our youth. Be it drugs, poverty, or violence—any problem that surfaces in society is sure to leave a mark on kids and in schools, and schools must respond. Districts can no longer focus solely on the three R's when these disturbing trends are absorbed (Stratton, 10).

What is needed is a proactive approach. Social services must be expanded and at the same time consolidated to ensure they're delivered in the most efficient manner. East Hartford High School may have found the right blend with an emphasis on prevention with its Student Assistance Center (SAC).

East Hartford, Connecticut, is a suburban town in the midst of absorbing a growing number of residents newly arrived from its urban neighbor, Hartford. Families who have lived in town for generations live and work with families recently arrived in the town or in the country. A very diverse mix of socioeconomic, ethnic, cultural, linguistic, and educational levels exists.

An unassuming suite of four rooms off the school's library, East Hartford High School's SAC is the first stop for students whose arguments are threatening to escalate. It is the home base for 12-step meetings and for group and individual counseling. It is a resource for teachers and parents who see kids in trouble, or just heading that way. In its first year in existence, it reduced the number of suspensions and detentions in the school by 44 percent.

Violence prevention and conflict resolution are both a school and community effort. Early intervention is an essential component of prevention. Parents, students, teachers, and administrators—all must do their part in ridding our public schools of violence. On the front line are the teachers.

The Educator's Role and Responsibility

Without exception, classroom teachers can make a difference in ridding our schools of violence, and reinforcing the mission of the SAC and the peacekeeping, negotiation strategies taught there. But each of us must do his or her part.

Not only must we ask our students questions, we must take the time to listen and to hear what they are saying. Even what may seem like idle threats need to be taken at face value and reported to administration as well as to parents. Often teachers are afraid to interfere with parenting. It is our responsibility to recognize our partnership with parents and to contact them when appropriate.

One commonality in the profile of school shooters is a feeling of isolation, observes Harvard Medical School clinical psychologist Robert Brooks in *Time* (Sullivan, 35). Our role as teachers requires us to be vigilant, making referrals to guidance counselors or social workers when a student appears troubled or alienated. We cannot afford to ignore or trivialize a child's pain at being teased or excluded. That old "sticks and stones" adage is wrong; names do hurt. Bullies cannot be tolerated in our classes, nor should deliberate meanness in any form—including exclusion—be allowed.

A focus on inclusion can help each child feel that his or her participation and contribution are valued and that he or she belongs. We must work to build healthy self-esteem, so necessary for becoming happy, socialized people.

In the classroom, negotiation skills are taught through the use of cooperative learning groups, where students learn how to provide positive feedback and tactful, constructive criticism. Here teachers can help students develop standards and apply them. It is also here where students should be encouraged to look for the good rather than focus on the negative. Most important, cooperative learning groups provide practice in group problem solving, finding common ground, and reaching compromise.

Cooperative learning can be most successful when the teacher assigns each student to a specific role to play within each group, ideally matching student strengths to the tasks required. In English class, for example, for the purpose of literary discussion, the popular "literature circles" approach assigns students to some variations of roles like summarizer, questioner, illuminator, illustrator, and vocabulary developer. With group tasks structured to promote active participation and to help students meet success within their range of abilities, students build self-esteem as they share credit for the group's success.

As an active, contributing member of this type of *ad hoc* "clique," the student's productivity, self-control, and confidence rise through expanded opportunities for participation with his or her peers in class. By learning through cooperative group work that the whole is only as good as the sum of its parts, students gain experience using life skills and developing a sense of shared responsibility. Cooperative learning is one of our most effective teaching strategies and it reinforces those skills promoted in the SAC.

Whether the teacher chooses to use pairing-and-sharing or cooperative groups, this student-centered learning environment fosters greater understanding of and empathy for individual difference; most students discover through the process that everyone has something to contribute. No one ever needs to be excluded.

Language arts, social studies, and contemporary issues teachers have the perfect forum for teaching students how to resolve differences peacefully. By being introduced to the rules and strategies of public debate and activities like mock trials and role-playing, students learn the rudiments of making and keeping peace. By exploring the precise use of language in debate and discussion, kids learn to settle disputes outside of school without violence using the same techniques.

Teachers must be willing to take the time from academic tasks to pursue teachable moments on ethics and values. Too many opportunities are missed because of fear of being off-task. We may never get a second chance.

These are tangible ways teachers can help control conflict before it starts.

Note the synergy in these two statements: Students who have self-control and can accept differences are less apt to resort to violence; a safe school permits students to learn and acquire these valuable skills. Each of these goals needs the other.

Sticks and Stones: Mean-Free Classrooms

Some critics of public education claim that high schools today have lost their focus. Bard College President Leo Botstein
recently indicted public schools as "sports dominated and clique
driven," operating in a social culture distorted by the "artificial
popularity" created by cliques and obscuring the educational focus of our nation's schools (Botstein, 2000).

In considering how to create a safe and tolerant school environment, we cannot underrate the hurtfulness of name-calling and
other bullying behaviors. Anyone who has been on the receiving
end knows that while it may not show, it hurts. Students who
have been picked on know this anguish too well. How many teachers have tried to console students who have been the target of
name-calling? Girls who have been called "hos" (slang for "whore")
are frequently unable to return their focus on class work. Many
times it is the "smart" or the "good" student who is targeted,
unless he or she is also an athlete or particularly attractive or char-
ismatic. They are called "geeks" or "nerds." Some of them with-
draw from social life and become loners. Others who are picked
on may wear suggestive clothing or odd, ghoulish garb, or suffer
from extreme shyness, which can be misconstrued as rudeness or
arrogance. Some are just, in some unnamable way, different.

They all know that old saying about sticks and stones is wrong.
Being teased causes an intense psychic pain that cannot be escaped,
and it is especially damaging during the difficult teen and adolescent years when children are developing and exploring what will
become their adult selves. Of course, neither parenting nor peer
influence alone can be blamed for school tragedies. But name-
calling and other harassment by classmates—especially if unad-
dressed by teachers or other authority figures—is a common force
that has shaped many perpetrators of school violence.

The 15-year-old student who opened fire in March, 2001, in
Santee, California, killing two classmates and wounding more than
a dozen others, was a victim of intense bullying and teasing. It
seems that everyone knew he was being mercilessly harassed; he
had nowhere to turn for help, and nobody intervened. He even

made open threats, but they were ignored. Similarly, the two shoot-ers in Littleton, Colorado, who killed 15 people and injured al-most two dozen others in April, 1999, were outsiders, considered "unpopular." They too gave explicit signs of their plans. At Santana High School, the 15-year-old shooter told more than a dozen people of his plan (Bower, 31).

No one should tolerate hurtful teasing or be made to feel ostracized or alienated. To head off problems before they start, teachers can help by maintaining what some educational research-ers call "mean-free" classrooms, where bullying and teasing are not allowed. Educators can create an environment where all stu-dents feel they have something to contribute, and that those con-tributions are valued. Teachers must refer persistent bullys to the principal, the SAC, or its counterpart, where they can get adult intervention to head off any potential problems before matters go too far.

Other students suffer from a more private pain. Some who perform well in class, who are quiet and do not act out, suffer psychic pain or personal problems that frequently go unnoticed, contributing to feelings of alienation. It becomes painfully appar-ent to front-line teachers who these isolates are. They sit by them-selves or with other members of the social fringe at lunch, or they skip lunch to lean against walls outside the cafeteria—alone.

For others, a painful shyness keeps them from reaching out. Even some "good" students have difficulty sharing personal prob-lems. For many, to do so would acknowledge that the problems are real. And reality can hurt. They remain on the outside, their exclusion contributing to feelings of despair.

In many classrooms, the disruptive students, those usurping learning time, are the ones who monopolize the teacher's atten-tion. This is not acceptable. ZERO tolerance for meanness and name-calling extends to disruptive behavior as well.

Each of these situations—name calling, bullying, disruptive students, the quiet and overt cries for attention from students—can be addressed by a flexible and functioning SAC. Teachers can make referrals that will allow the Student Assistant Team to reach out to the student and find an appropriate resource.

We cannot accept teacher (or peer) oversight and inaction that allows students in need to slip between the cracks unnoticed. It's time to take out the caulking gun.

Assertive Parenting

The lines of communication between home and school should be wide open, with both sides feeling comfortable about raising and discussing issues. Parents and teachers are invaluable to each other, and the absence of active parenting is a major problem. Time has been eroded by the work schedules of both parents and their kids. Parents are being torn between maintaining their jobs and actively participating in their children's lives. Many students who discussed teen life in their English class with a *Hartford Courant* reporter recently, nodded in agreement at one senior's description of family interaction today:

> When kids get in, you go get your plate, and go straight to your room. Nobody has time to set up the table and enjoy a meal, and talk about your daily problems. The thing of having dinner every night and having the whole family sit down and talk is over. This is a new day and age where people are on the go. You get some McDonald's and you keep stepping. (Megan, D4)

For parents, knowing their child also means knowing when to seek help. Instances of bullying or hurtful teasing can undermine educators' and parents' best efforts. Parents, like teachers, need to take these seriously. These problems, and any others that parents feel are beyond their ability to deal with alone, must not be ignored and should be reported to the school. Schools are partners in the parenting process and can help find solutions. Parents must be made familiar with the services and support offered by the SAC, not in an atmosphere of blame, but with all efforts extended cooperatively towards solving the problems.

While many parents do try hard and are actively involved in their children's lives, some blame the school's disciplinary woes on weak administrative enforcement of rules and a lack of alternative programs for those students who just don't fit in or who cannot adjust to the public school structure. Parent and teachers alike condemn the lack of consistent enforcement of school discipline policies.

Administrators, on the other hand, complain that the parents of troubled kids don't back them up when their children act out at school. A principal who suspends a child for violence or inappropriate behavior is clearly having a very limited impact when that child's parent—sometimes in the presence of the student—defiantly defends his child's behavior and belittles the school's discipline.

Many young people have too much unmonitored time alone or with the wrong people, with no one to talk to and no one to just listen. Many have too much time to nurture grudges and ruminate about past injustices, too much time to plot revenge.

Society can no longer accept absentee or *laissez-faire* parenting. Parents have an obligation to know what their children are up to and with whom. They must listen more and talk less. A proactive approach to parenting must be adopted. Parents need to monitor their children's alone time.

While parents must be able to treat their children as they would treat any person—with respect and consideration—they must be willing to say no when a choice is not in a child's best interest. Good parenting means setting limits, whether it be the amount of time the child spends playing video games, surfing the Internet, or watching television. Children whose parents do set limits such as curfews, and wait up for them to come home, say they like it because they know they are loved. Children who do not have curfews or are left unmonitored, while they like the fact that their parents trust them, express envy for those whose parents take that extra interest to check on them or to lose their own sleep to make sure their child returns home safely.

Parents need not be afraid of asking too many questions. Questions reflect interest. For those who worry about appearing too nosey or prying, not only is it your right to ask, it is your responsibility as a parent to know.

Years ago, it was the guidance department that would have taken the brunt of the blame for those human catastrophes of violence. But today's guidance counselors are so overwhelmed with scheduling, test scores, graduation credits, and college recommendations that little time is left over for old-fashioned guidance, even for the more troubled or at-risk students or those who are just afraid to graduate.

In many schools, it is the guidance departments and the arts that were most ravaged by the layoffs of the '80s. Just maybe we are now beginning to face the long-term consequences. Maybe it's time to turn the business of guiding our youth back to the guidance department and to put other preventative or support programs in place. Regardless, an SAC is one weapon in dealing with conflict and many other problems faced by students every day.

For parents and educators alike, the words of a speaker at the funeral of one of the young victims of the Columbine tragedy should remain indelible: "Somewhere in the reach of every adult in this country is a child to hold and teach, a child to save." (Pagnozzi, 1999)

What Can Administrators Do?

Conflict can be debilitating to even the most efficient public schools—devastating morale, teamwork, self-esteem, and ultimately crippling the productivity of our students. There are no quick fixes for the crisis in our public schools. For most districts, a combination of approaches works best in keeping violence in check and conflict under control. Everyone must assume some responsibility for making our schools safe. While the needs of every school and every district will be a little bit different, core elements of an SAC or other preventative programs apply everywhere.

Good administrators are also good motivators who urge their teachers and staff to go above and beyond—to reach out to kids. Pioneering resilience researcher Julius Segal and other psychologists agree that to build resilience, children need to develop a "linchpin relationship" with some parental figure—someone a child can identify with and garner strength from.

Another tangible way good administrators can respond proactively in heading off conflict is to encourage greater focus on character education. This includes placing greater emphasis on manners, social graces, tact, and diplomacy.

Outside the classroom, administrators need to find a greater variety of acceptable activities, beyond athletics, both extracurricular and cocurricular, to appeal to a broader spectrum of student interests. For some students, particularly those with limited athletic abilities, the pressure of competition is so intimidating that they do not even try out for competitive sports. The inclusion of a wider selection of noncompetitive activities greatly expands opportunities for student involvement, creativity, and success, thereby enhancing students' sense of belonging, building self-esteem and complementing the SAC's goals.

Administrators play a critical role. They must be highly visible to staff and students; they set the tone for the school. The days of the phantom administrator are gone. It is crucial that administrators are out in the school, experiencing students and activities first hand, making connections, building trust, and inviting confidences, as well as ensuring that school policies are implemented effectively.

Through their high visibility, administrators can work to disperse cliques before they can assume power or become a threat— whether physically or emotionally—to the well being of those who are on the outside. They can also serve to motivate teachers and other staff and to emphasize the importance of prevention to the school community. By taking prevention seriously, the principal empowers teachers and students to take it seriously as well.

East Hartford High School and the Student Assistance Center

East Hartford High School has worked hard to develop a healthy balance of safety measures and proactive programs, such as the Student Assistance Center (SAC), to help keep our schools free of violence and our children safe. It is a model with proven results supported by impressive statistics. In the SAC's first year alone, the school experienced a 44 percent reduction in suspensions and detentions.

East Hartford is an urban community with an increasingly mobile population of approximately 55,000 inhabitants, and is a microcosm of the nation's social ills. It borders the city of Hartford and is halfway between New York City and Boston. The high school has a cultural blend of students from more than 70 countries around the globe. In the hallways you can hear more than 50 languages spoken. It is a veritable melting pot. While the cultural mix is one of the school's strengths, it has also brought with it many challenges.

Conflict is part of life, and it can increase with rapid social change, but conflict need not lead to violence, as East Hartford High School's Student Assistance Center program has proven.

As the nation as a whole becomes more fragmented and violent, public schools need to become more adept at addressing the challenges that arise from our constantly changing social atmosphere and landscape.

The highly successful introduction of the SAC has helped East Hartford High School establish an environment in which violence, and many behaviors that can lead to it, are not tolerated. East Hartford is a community in transition, facing all of challenges that confront the urban centers in our nation. When the High School High School SAC was born, the Student Assistance Team approach was being used on a limited basis in two elementary schools in town with encouraging results. At East Hartford High, the only high school in the city, the SAC has evolved into a truly indispensable intervention medium.

This program offers other schools and districts a practical approach for dealing with social and cultural changes, conflict resolution, and violence prevention. Many aspects of the SAC have been replicated in numerous communities nationally with positive outcomes. The lessons of East Hartford's SAC apply to schools and to students everywhere.

Chapter 2

Start Up
Beginnings Are Not Easy

Support from the Top and from Your School
A Committee to Reflect the Community
Student Input: A New Imperative
The Director
Staffing and Interns
The SAC's Backbone: The Student Assistance Team
Logistics: Finding the Right Space
Making Connections

Τhe Student Assistance Center (SAC) is a tangible demonstration of the school's commitment to helping students work out their problems so they may better function academically. It is a proactive approach to violence prevention. This chapter outlines how to create such a program and to foster a school environment where violence is not tolerated and does not develop. These methods are offered merely as a guide. The components of an SAC should be modified to best meet the unique needs of each community. Chapter 8 provides some overview of funding.

The SAC is made up of many support and enrichment programs, all of which are coordinated and, ideally, centrally located. Programs can include peer mediation, drug and alcohol counseling, conflict resolution, violence prevention, social work, multicultural activities, groups aimed at assisting students in college and career choices, and other types of mediation. Chapters 5 and 6 give ideas of some of the programs and services of the SAC.

A Student Assistance Team or SAT, is made up of teachers and other interested school staff who triage students referred to the SAC by holding an initial meeting to identify issues and resources. Each school's SAC will be different, based on the needs of the students and the community as identified in a Needs-Assessment Survey (see Appendix 2).

Support from the Top and from Your School

Before the objectives of a Student Assistance Center concept can be sold to its publics, the project must have the backing of school administration and faculty. (See Appendix 1 for a Timeline.) This support is essential to meeting the basic requirements of an SAC, including assigning staff and resources and appropriating office space to house the center. Even more importantly, strong support from the top is extremely helpful in sustaining the fledgling program, giving it the time and direction needed to develop and evolve.

Similarly, faculty support is needed to help educate students about the multi-faceted role of the SAC, as well as to help run the center and to recruit staff to serve on its Student Assistance Team. In garnering support for the SAC, founders stressed that while problems in schools can be overwhelming, every member of the school community must contribute to the development of a collaborative educational environment:

> The task of the school is to educate students and prepare them to move successfully into their chosen career path. When issues such as substance abuse, suicide, or living in a dysfunctional family occur in a child's life, they often interfere with the educational process. It then becomes necessary for school personnel to assist in resolving these issues so that the learning process can be facilitated. This does not mean that educators will become therapists. (Casale, 1992, 9)

The SAC is a viable new-style structure that can meet these social and educational demands, and this must be communicated to parents, faculty, administrators, and to students.

In East Hartford, the SAC occupies four rooms at one of two entrances to the school's library (see Appendix 3). Its separate rooms allow privacy when needed, while its central location near the heart of the school makes it easy for students and staff to drop by. Your SAC may not have as many rooms; you may be able to set aside only a small office or a large vacant classroom. Any space for an SAC is better than none, and can serve as a place for your program to germinate and grow.

A Committee to Reflect the Community

At the outset, a steering committee should be created to shape and develop the SAC. It should be made up of political officials, clergy, faculty, school administrators, students, parents, and possibly law enforcement officials. The goal is to establish a group that is a microcosm of the community. Helping plan and form your program gives members of this committee a stake in its success, and brings outside resources to enrich the SAC. Ultimately, this committee will become a valuable mediating tool as well as an essential political ally. Keep your steering committee involved once your program is underway. Running an effective SAC requires the support of all members of the school community—administration, faculty, parents, and students.

Ideally, the SAC should facilitate communication within the school community to better meet the needs of the school's population. The SAC is responsible for keeping the lines of communication open among groups so that they can work together. For this to happen, community involvement should be a goal from the outset (see Timeline, Appendix 1). A combination of approaches offers the best opportunities for conveying the SAC message and generating support, including volunteers for the Student Assistance Team:

- Presentations at staff meetings
- Staff bulletins
- SAC newsletters
- School and district newsletters
- Print media and special events
- Student orientations
- Information booths at events
- Involvement in community organizations
- Student newspapers
- Chamber of Commerce newsletters
- Other community groups

In addition to contemporaneous inter-school referrals of students in need, a list of referrals should be compiled at the end of the school year by the middle schools to alert the high school about middle-school students heading into high school who may need help adjusting to the new school environment (see Appendix 12). This "alert list" should be broken down and assigned to SAT members at the beginning of the school year so that identified freshmen can form a connection with a concerned staff member and get to know where to go for help before a problem arises.

Student Input: A New Imperative

Giving students a decision-making role in their school, and the authority and responsibility to handle their own problems, puts an entirely different slant on things. This student input and authority are critical to the success of East Hartford's SAC.

Students cannot thrive in school if their day-to-day consciousness is clouded with issues not associated with school. Feelings of alienation, problems resulting from parents' divorce, toxic home lives, or other outgrowths of unsatisfactory relationships are all challenges the SAC programs can help overcome.

To the student, the SAC serves as a catchall, a safe haven, a place to go in the face of problems that appear insurmountable. Therefore, to design an appropriate program, the particular needs of the students must first be identified. A formal assessment device is called for at this point.

To determine the relative severity and frequency of common teenage problems and dilemmas in your community, distribute a Needs-Assessment Survey (Appendix 2) to a representative sample of the school population. This essential information should serve to mold the program into its own unique form, reflecting both student and community needs, and provides some of the absolutely necessary contributions from those who know best what is happening in the students' lives—the students themselves.

The first step in designing your Needs-Assessment Survey is to think about distinct categories of disturbances in the lives of these youth. Some SAC issues center on school problems, but many conflicts brew overnight and are brought into the school from home. Name-calling, gossip, rumors, jealousy, sexual orientation and relationship issues, family disputes, sibling rivalry, displaced hostilities, abandoned friendships, and shattered trust—the SAC is an appropriate forum for students to work through raw emotion and these potentially volatile issues with an impartial third party. The Needs-Assessment Survey questions are aimed at assessing student needs in the overarching problems of violence, drug and alcohol abuse, pregnancy, suicide, issues of race, gender, and sexual orientation.

The larger issues are clear: Nationally, 23 percent of children five years old and under live below the poverty line (Belcher 1995); 24 percent of minors live with only one parent; the United States has the dubious distinction of leading the industrialized world in teenage pregnancy; and suicide is the second leading killer of people aged 14 to 25 (Cooley 1993). The Needs-Assessment Survey will help you focus you efforts to best serve your community.

The Director

The director of the Student Assistance Center must be someone with strong interpersonal skills who demonstrates a blend of charisma, knowledge, and experience. A full-time director is ideal, but a part-time one may be necessary to get started, and, depending on the school's needs, may serve you well for some time.

The director's position is multifaceted. He or she may be called upon to interview new staff, develop a budget, secure fiscal stability, write grants, develop new programs, and coordinate existing ones.

The director's role is that of bridge-builder between various segments of the school community, including administrators, teachers, guidance counselors, nurses, parents, and students. Because of these numerous demands, it is very helpful if the director's time and position are not shared by another discipline or other assigned duties. The center's director must be perceived as neutral by all parties involved. Any semblance of bias could spell disaster.

Staffing and Interns

In addition to a director and any specialists, such as social workers and drug and alcohol counselors, working out of the

Student Assistance Center, the SAC staff consists of teacher volunteers. Many of the best teachers volunteer to participate in the Student Assistance Team, which allows for teachers and troubled students to interact one-on-one. Teachers freely volunteer to spend free periods staffing the center.

Some schools serve as Professional Development Centers for universities and thus are fortunate to have graduate interns further staff the SAC. Local colleges and universities can often provide qualified and competent interns. This, like peer mediation itself, provides both participants—the program and the interns— with a win-win situation, for both tend to grow through this mutually beneficial, symbiotic relationship.

When selecting a five-day college intern, choose one to complement the director. The interns should mirror the population that uses the Student Assistance Center in terms of gender, ethnicity, sexual orientation, and other factors. Proper balance of gender is important. Just a fact to note: in East Hartford, more than 75 percent of the students seen in the SAC are female. While it is typically males who resort to violence, girls appear more willing to seek intervention before the problems escalate to the physical level. Choose your staff with discretion.

The SAC's Backbone:
The Student Assistance Team

A Student Assistance Team (SAT) is made up of teachers, security workers, guidance counselors, school nurses, school social workers, and SAC staff members. The objective of an SAT is to triage staff immediately with troubled students and arrange direct contact when needed between students, faculty, or other resources outside of the classroom. Further goals include prevention and intervention, as well as the referral of students to additional services, as the need arises.

The SAT system operates under the belief that students function better in school when they form connections with other people in that community.

A Student Assistance Team works by first identifying students who would benefit from adult intervention. A locked box with referral forms (Appendix 8) is placed in a central location such as the main office, so that faculty members may recommend appropriate students. Possible causes for referral might include deteriorating academic performance, high incidents of disciplinary infractions, cutting class, and truancy.

Referred students are matched to an SAT member, who meets with the student to learn more about the problem and devise an intervention to help alleviate it. (See Intake Form, Appendix 10.) The SAT member who takes on the case should apprise the person who made the initial referral of the outcome, and check back with both the student and the referring party in about six weeks to update the situation. Some members of the SAT should also be assigned solely to the duty of follow-up on interventions. (See SAC Reply Form, Appendix 11.)

In some cases, SAT members are needed merely to serve as mentors. The social work staff may be employed for in-house training on sensitivity, intake skills, and identification of student problems.

Student Assistance Center program specialists noted that the ideal composition of an SAT is a cross-section of staff:

> The typical [SAC] has a Student Assistance Team that includes a substance abuse specialist and representatives from the key units in the school. The composition of this team includes faculty representatives, administrators involved in student discipline, and counselors addressing teenage academic and social development in the school setting. (Moore and Foster, 1993)

In East Hartford, many teachers willingly use free periods to work in the SAC. As faculty members assigned to the SAC, they become part of the SAT, but while in the SAC they function as one-to-one counselors for students other than their own. While some staff members are assigned to the SAC in lieu of supervision duty and by special arrangement, other teachers typically drop in during their conference periods or after school. The synergistic approach furnishes the appropriate setting for the teacher-student relationship to be fine-tuned. Teachers have the satisfaction of knowing they can have an impact. An SAC volunteer receives the intrinsic reward of knowing that he or she has made a difference in a student's life.

The student/SAT member relationship has created numerous life-long bonds. It is because the "staff" of the SAT is not made up of just teachers—it includes administrators, interns, and security officers, as well as students who are involved in this process. All members of the SAT are greatly affected by the success of the program.

The potential for interpersonal bonds was illustrated recently. An SAT member met with a referred freshman on several occasions but had no luck connecting. In the teacher's last scheduled meeting with the student, an object dropped out of the student's backpack. What was the object? A baseball card, which was the start of a great friendship. The teacher was a collector of cards, as was the student. A baseball card club was formed, with the teacher being the advisor and the student being the president.

When establishing an SAT, inexperienced teacher volunteers may need direction. If your school is large enough, groups or clusters of SAT members should be formed with at least one member of each cluster having experience counseling students as a guidance counselor, social worker, nurse, or SAC staff member. Regular classroom teachers involved in the SAT will grow in this area as a result of interaction with these counseling professionals.

Communication among SAT members is especially important. Meetings should be held periodically, at least once a term, to concentrate on what has been accomplished and what can be improved, and what new directions the team may need to take in the future. Ideally, each cluster should organize biweekly meetings. (See Appendix 7 for an overview of SAT procedures.)

Generally, SAT members do not receive extra pay or free time for their SAT duties. Ideally, the SAT is large enough so that the duties don't overburden individual teachers. In East Hartford, with about 140 teachers and 2,500 students, there are 40 members of the SAT. Student Assistance Team members meet with referred students between five and 10 times a year. For such a minimal time commitment, the potential to make a huge impact on a young person's life is tremendous.

Logistics: Finding the Right Space

Logistics is a very important issue. The Student Assistance Center should not be perceived as a "second-class citizen." It is most effective when in an area that is accessible to all parties involved. It has to be user-friendly, yet it must offer enough privacy to deal with sensitive issues (see Appendix 3).

East Hartford's SAC consists of a suite of four rooms: one administrative and three for break-out rooms used for isolation, negotiations, or mediation. This has worked out extremely well. While your school may not have a suite available, it is essential to house any component in a user-friendly environment. What student would seek help in a room adjacent to the boiler room or in a closet commandeered from the custodians? Who is comfortable talking about intimate personal problems in an office that is separated from others by a flimsy divider that doesn't allow for a private conversation?

Many schools do not have extra space for nonacademic programs, but the overall need for violence prevention and creating a healthy school climate must be considered. At the very least, an SAC needs a private mediation room situated so that it does not interfere with the school's academic programs. If a suite of rooms is not available, whatever space is available will get you started. Once a program gets underway, people will see its value and more space may become available.

Making Connections

From the outset, the Student Assistance Center model, to grow and evolve, needs the support of agencies outside of the school that operate on national, state, and local levels. Staff is encouraged to attend workshops and conferences to secure information and support from outside experts. Qualified, well-informed assistance from outside of the school community helps the program improve and grow. Outside agencies can also provide information and assistance in forming and implementing the different facets of the program.

Regardless of whether they elect to become staff mediators or SAT members or not, regular classroom teachers are especially important in preventing conflict and violence. They are on the front line, and we depend upon them to notice the problems students may be having and to refer these students to the SAC. Therefore, garnering the support of both the teachers and nonprofessional staff is necessary to the function of the SAC. (See Chapter 7, "Winning Your Public.")

The Student Assistance Center in East Hartford works together with the students, faculty, and community. The program's plan is a collaborative effort of agencies and has spawned several other preventative programs in the school and community, including:

- ⮣ Peer Mediation Training K-6
- ⮣ Police Outreach
- ⮣ On-Site Adult Probation
- ⮣ Cultural Enrichment
- ⮣ YMCA Teen Center
- ⮣ Child Plan Forum

Educators should take a proactive approach by getting as many students as possible involved in the SAC's many programs.

Once the program is established, try to remain in contact with these outside agencies in a continuous spirit of renewal. Continue extending and sharing the successes and experiences with other programs and schools. To open lines of communication and opportunity, SAC directors should serve on and be active in as many agency boards as possible so that others may be inspired and reap the benefit from these unique experiences.

It is essential to open up and sustain a dialog between agencies to ensure that a program does not become stagnant. As society changes, schools must also change. Currently, 10 special-needs groups meet weekly out of East Hartford's SAC suites. That number continues to grow.

Chapter 3

Mediations
Empowering Students

Types of Mediations: Peer, Self, and Staff
The Mediation Process
Selecting Mediators
Mediation Training
The Peer Mediation Process
Using the Mediation System: Violence Prevention at Work

Conflict resolution and violence prevention through mediation are the mainstays of the Student Assistance Center. Some issues that come to the SAC are the outgrowth of the school day, such as academic problems, conflicts over rumors, insults, hurtful teasing, and failed friendships. Others brew overnight and are brought to school from home. They emanate from phone fights, boyfriend-girlfriend issues, and parent, peer, or sibling disputes. The SAC offers a neutral turf to defuse these potentially explosive issues. W. DeJong stresses the optimal atmosphere for conflict resolution:

> Conflict resolution is best taught in a caring community characterized by cooperation, effective communication, emotional strength, appreciation of difference, recognition of common purposes, and shared decision-making. (DeJong, 1993)

Mediation has proved an extremely effective tool in solving conflicts *before they become violent*. By interrupting a situation before it escalates, students are empowered to solve their own problems—and they are given the tools to do so.

Once the first punch is thrown, the incident no longer calls for mediation: instead, disciplinary measures must be pursued. But successful mediations reduce the use of traditional school disciplinary measures such as detentions, suspensions, and expulsions by solving problems before they reach the point of requiring the intervention of the school administration.

Types of Mediation: Peer, Self, and Staff

Three types of mediation should be made available in the SAC: peer, staff, and self-mediation.

With peer mediation, three trained student mediators are brought together with the disputants and a non-participating adult observer. The three mediators are selected for each mediation on the basis of experience, gender, and ethnicity so that the needs of the specific disputants are most effectively met. With staff mediation, a trained teacher or school worker facilitates the process. In self-mediation, students are given space and guidelines to resolve their own problems.

Despite the 99 percent success rate of peer mediation, it is self-mediation that perhaps enjoys the most remarkable results. But it's only appropriate that certain types of relatively minor disputes, usually occurring between students who have been friends and wish to continue to be friends, be handled this way. More volatile circumstances demand staff mediation.

To prevent violence, it's critical to take threats seriously. Staff mediation or conflict resolution is called for in disputes that have gone too far, when excessive raw emotion is in evidence, or where physical violence is imminent if the situation is not defused. Others may be asked to help in this peacekeeping effort. Adult SAC staff members, security guards, assistant principals, and police officers who are familiar with the issues and respected by the community may be called upon to resolve especially volatile arguments.

Career Mediation Inc. lists the following types of conflicts as appropriate for mediation:

- Rumors, gossip
- Name-calling, bullying
- Turf issues (i.e., lockers and personal property)
- Cafeteria problems
- Boyfriend/girlfriend issues
- "Near fights"
- Intolerance of difference
- Jealousy

The Mediation Process

The mediation process has several stages. Staff and student mediators are thoroughly trained to work through all six steps.

Stage 1—All disputants are present. Ground rules are established: confidentiality, respect, no interruptions.

Stage 2—Disputants each have uninterrupted time to tell their side of the story.

Stage 3—Mediators identify the problems and summarize the main points.

Stage 4—Disputants get a chance to suggest ways to solve their problems.

Stage 5—Mediators help the disputants evaluate the proposed solutions and select one or more alternatives that work for all participants involved.

Stage 6—Mediators write the agreement (the Career Mediation, Inc. agreement form is provided in Appendix 5). It is then signed by all participants. In the contract, the disputants basically agree to stop arguing or fighting through any means they deem necessary, i.e., not talking to or about each other in the future.

During any mediation, mediators, staff members, or disputants can call a "time out" for the purposes of:

☐ Discussing strategies
☐ Resolving issues apart from the mediation
☐ Clearing up questions
☐ Stopping the process for cooling down
☐ Removing disputants
☐ Involving additional individuals in the mediation process

Selecting Mediators

The first step in the formation of a mediation program is selecting mediators.

Prospective peer mediators are chosen from the complete spectrum of students. Be sure to include all of the subgroups making up the school population. This affords a closer match in the composition of the mediation panel to mirror that of the disputants in grade level, gender, and ethnicity. This also makes it easier for the peer mediation program to be accepted as a positive process and prevents it from being viewed as "uncool." No one subset should be able to dominate the balance in mediator selection. Some of our mediators are honor students, some are athletes, some may even be seen as "negative leaders," those who are revered for less than honorable reasons. The key is that all of these students have some kernel of leadership that can be tapped.

Recommendations for peer mediators can be sought from the assistant principals, the guidance office, the faculty and the students themselves. Once recommended, these students complete both an application and a questionnaire about their activities, attitudes, and leadership potential. A sample application is offered in Appendix 6. In addition, interviews of selected students takes place before training to ascertain their level of commitment. After SAC staff reviews the questionnaires, peer mediators are chosen for training.

Mediation Training

Everyone involved in mediation—staff, administrators, students, and community members—will undergo training. Initially, each session should have 15 to 20 actively involved individuals, with no observers. While methodology may vary, most programs typically include role-playing, instruction on group dynamics, listening skills, interviewing techniques, and effective questioning skills. In East Hartford, we've found that approximately 20 hours of training broken up into six to eight three-hour sessions works better than all-day sessions. Most students' attention starts to wane after lunch break.

Topics covered in training include conflict resolution styles, active listening skills, open and closed questions, bias awareness, dealing with anger, and the mediation process itself. Role-playing is a technique used extensively in these training sessions. With the proper warm-up, most participants easily get into role-playing and enjoy the experience.

Before newly SAC-trained students can start taking part in mediations, they sit on a panel with two or more seasoned mediators for their first few mediations to gain experience. All peer mediators receive refresher training during the year.

The final link in the training chain is the in-service training of the school staff. Staff mediators attend workshops and continually update their skills.

Not all staff members or students are suited for the mediation process. Mediators must be calm, flexible, and optimistic. They should be able to adapt to any situation and to interact effectively with others within the high school and the community.

Initially, an outside agency should be selected to train both staff members and students. However, by the end of the first year, individuals will step forward and express an interest in becoming trainers themselves.

As the SAC gets underway and develops a track record, videos, written texts, and other resource materials should be collected and cataloged for use in continuing education. Mediation training is an ongoing educational process that becomes refined and streamlined with time. The SAC will become a repository for this and other information.

The Peer Mediation Process

The mediation process itself starts with disputants meeting with a three-student panel; with three mediators, the stress is not on the shoulders of only one individual. Psychologically, it also creates an atmosphere of dominance—three mediators vs. two disputant.

Once an agreement has been reached (see "The Mediation Process," above), it is then recorded in the disputants' own words and reviewed by the mediators. The agreement is signed by all parties—mediators, disputants, and faculty observers—at the conclusion of each mediation. The contract is then filed for future reference, if needed. (See sample agreement form in Appendix 5.)

Mediations may occur at any time. Students are encouraged to refer themselves to the mediation process; they can also be referred by other students, administrators, teachers, or other staff, as well as collaborative community agencies (see Chapter 6, "Support Services and Agencies"). They may also be referred by a parent who suspects his or her child is being teased or otherwise harassed or is experiencing other social difficulties.

A typical peer mediation process might proceed as follows:

1. An administrator, teacher, staff, student, parent, or individual makes a referral to the SAC.

2. The disputants are brought to the SAC and isolated (in separate rooms, if possible).

3. Three mediators are located immediately. (Don't wait—schedules are in a folder.) Find the best fit (gender, grade, race, ethnic background).

4. Brief the mediators on the issues.

5. After a cooling-off period, bring the disputants into the mediation room simultaneously, never separately.

    a. One vs. One (preferred)

       Two vs. Two (occasionally)

       Two vs. One (never)

    b. If there are other students involved—isolate them and rotate. Example: Students who are referred usually appear at the SAC with a friend.

    c. Seat the disputants on opposite sides of the room.

6. The three mediators take charge of the process, with the faculty or staff acting as observer, sitting in a neutral location.

7. At the end of the mediation, an agreement is recorded and the "contract" is signed.

Closure takes place in 99 percent of all mediations. For the sake of follow-up and for record-keeping, a file should be maintained on all successful mediations. Also, keep on file all agreements for the remaining one percent not mediated. Usually follow-up calls to the disputants' homes that night are helpful, as well as a second follow-up a few days later.

In East Hartford, the SAC handles more than 200 disputes each year. If the disputants cannot reach an agreement, which is typical in just one percent of cases, more traditional measures are taken to solve the problem: assistant principals are involved, parents are notified, disciplinary action is taken, and students are sent home for a cooling-off period.

Using the Mediation System: Violence Prevention at Work

Students may not just drop in and hang out in the SAC. Those not assigned to the SAC as mediators or student workers must have a valid pass to seek services from the center.

Once trained mediators are in place, establish systems for referral and scheduling procedures. Publicize the service and encourage all interested parties to make use of it. Teachers, administrators, parents, and the students themselves should be encouraged to make referrals. In the wake of the Columbine and Santana massacres, the latter takes on particular significance. Everyone is responsible for keeping schools safe. While it may go against the unwritten code of silence that one does not "rat on" one's friends, the message the schools have to get across is that friends do take care of friends. The tragedy at Santana High School could have been prevented had friends stepped in. Particularly if there is potential for violence, students must take threats seriously, report hurtful teasing, or other potentially volatile situations.

Mediation must take place as soon as possible once a referral has been made. A copy of each peer mediator's schedule should be on hand in the SAC so that mediation can be efficiently arranged before or after class, during lunch, or whenever possible, during study halls. When this is not feasible, however, mediation can and should be scheduled during class periods. Better the loss of a part of a class than the required loss of several days of out-of-school suspension following a fight. Depending upon the size of the school, a large enough pool of mediators ensures ease of scheduling.

Referral forms (Appendix 8) provided by The Governor's Prevention Partnership should be distributed to encourage this practice, particularly at the program's inception. Once mediations start to take place, however, the program will gain a reputation that becomes self-perpetuating.

Mediations are often not the final chapter in a dispute. On many occasions, agreements are reopened for clarification of issues, re-negotiations of old issues, or infractions of the original agreement by one or both parties. Mediation contracts are kept on file at the SAC for just this purpose. Copies are not given to participants; the possibility of breaching confidentiality, and diminishing the effectiveness of that particular agreement and of the mediation process, is too great.

The reality is that most disputing parties will not "be themselves" that day, which will impact on how well they may or may not be able to function in class. This is when staff communication becomes so crucial. If the classroom teacher can be made aware of the possibility that the student may be having a difficult time and be kept apprised of the situation, the teacher will be less resentful of time "lost" to the SAC and can help to facilitate the student's successful return to normalcy.

Peer mediation is one of the most popular activities at East Hartford High School's SAC. Students who are involved in the mediation process, both as mediators and disputants, develop lifelong skills that they take with them into their communities.

Becoming a peer mediator helps instill a sense of pride and responsibility in the individual. As one student expressed to a *Hartford Courant* reporter, "You feel like you're doing a job. You're helping other people." (Ferguson, 1997, 2)

Chapter 4

Sample SAC Mediations and Student Interviews

SAC Mediations

Mediation 1—Cindy and Ana: Rumors

Mediation 2—Amanda and Chrissy: Betrayed Trust

Mediation 3—Ashley and Simone: Shared Locker

SAC Student Interviews

Interview 1—Darrell

Interview 2—Amber

Interview 3—Jamie

Interview 4—Luisa

Interview 5—Tanya

Interview 6—Jason

39

M any of the students who seek help from the SAC feel "disrespected" in some fashion. Females, in particular, are provoked by nonverbal gestures such as "She rolls her eyes at me" or "She sucks her teeth when I go by." For some, it is the people "getting up in my face" or "giving me attitude" that sets them off. The following is a sampling of the problems that have brought students to seek help from the SAC, in their words.

> A girl kept smacking my friend and I told her she'd better not hit him again. Then she wanted to fight me. So I went to the SAC with this guy. And she was called down to talk for the mediation. Then we talked it out.

> Me and my girl went to the SAC because this guy kept talking to my girl and wanting to get with her. I just wanted to get the truth to see if what I heard is true and tell him to keep away from my girl. She said nothing happened. He said nothing happened. He said he wouldn't bother her no more. Now I know nothing's going on.

> This girl felt I was disrespecting her. She gives me dirty looks all the time and whispers about me in algebra. I didn't even know why. In the SAC, we talk about it. She don't talk to me now, but she don't talk about me neither.

Many mediations conclude with a written contract, such as this one between two boys who had been provoking each other with names and rumors: "We agree to stay away from each other and not to say anything in the hallways and no confrontation."

SAC Mediations

Because of the emotionally charged atmosphere usually surrounding SAC matters, contentious parties are quickly assigned appropriate peer mediators who have been briefed on the nature of the dispute by the SAC director and are ushered into a small, private room. The mediators explain the ground rules. Then the disputants proceed, with each party explaining his or her side of the problem directly to the mediators, who clarify the facts and keep the mediation civil and focused. In this way, all mediators hear each disputant's side of the story first-hand, together. It is here that clarification is made and the facts are sorted.

The mediators then try to steer the disputants to suggest, evaluate, and select from alternatives, an agreement that all can live with. The agreement is put in writing and signed by all. The entire process usually can be wrapped up in less than a class period.

Excerpts from actual mediations are presented here, with names changed or deleted to maintain the privacy of those involved.

Mediation 1—Cindy and Ana: Rumors

Three mediators (M1, M2, and M3) introduce themselves and explain the ground rules. Before convening as a group, the disputants were separated so each party could share her side of the issue with a peer mediator. The mediation picks up from there:

M1: You have a problem you need to solve. You have to speak one at a time to us, not to each other. No name-calling, no swearing, no throwing stuff. You all can start. Why are you mad at her?

Cindy: I heard she is talking about me. I didn't want to go through all this. I just wanted to bring her up here so I could ask.

M1: She wants to know what was said, so you all don't want to beat down each other or anything like that?

Cindy: No, I want to know what was said. I can't swear and say her name. I heard she said I was a "B." How do I bleep words?

M1: We got that part, she call you—whatever.

Cindy: They were just saying some stuff about me.

Ana: Who are the "they?"

M2: She can't say who.

M1: You say you didn't say anything about Cindy?

Ana: I want to know who this other person is because I think she is lying. I want to confront this other person...

M2: She asked you up here to ask you. You don't want a [fight].

Cindy: No, I just wanted to ask her, but if you start saying something in the hall it turn into a big thing and everybody just wants a fight, and I didn't want that. I just wanted to bring her here to ask her. I don't want it to turn into *L.A. Law* or anything.

M2: (laughs) *L.A. Law.* So what's the agreement here?

Ana: What *is* the agreement?

M1: You've got to agree on something like, you all can't say stuff about each other behind each other's back.

Ana: Whoa, whoa. If you're speaking out for both of us that's a lie, 'cause we're gonna wind up saying something. That's a lie.

M1: Well I can't because, say, if she said something, and she came back here and said, "Ana was saying stuff about me," whatever, and if you got called back up here, you're gonna get in trouble. Your principals already know about this. Hope you know that.

Ana: Well, why is it turning...

M1: Your principals know about it every time you come here. Any time you have any mediation or anything, they know.

M2: So just agree on something. Can you leave this here? If you agree you don't want to get up in each other's face? You agree?

An agreement is written and signed by all parties present.

Mediation 2—Amanda and Chrissy: Betrayed Trust

Three mediators (M1, M2, M3) introduce themselves and explain the rules, after the parties had reconvened from meeting with mediators privately:

Chrissy: She was supposed to be my friend. Because of her, me and my boyfriend kind of broke up—not because of her, but I told her [a secret], because I thought she was my friend, and she told her best friend, Tracy, and Tracy told the whole school. I didn't come to school for two days because of it. I came back and confronted her and she got attitude with me. That's about it.

Amanda: The only reason I told my best friend was because

she asked about you two breaking up, because she kissed your man when you two were going out.

M1: Talk to us.

Chrissy: Well, if she was my friend she would have told me that before. She wouldn't have kept it to herself.

Amanda: That wasn't my place to tell. That was Tracy's place, which she was going to do if you came to school in those days.

M1: OK, so you are her best friend, and she told you it was a secret so why did you tell your other best friend?

Amanda: I don't know. I felt like it. She asked me if they were breaking up, and I told her they were arguing, and they broke up.

Chrissy: But I told her not to tell anybody, and she just goes right on and tells her best friend, and I don't think that's fair.

Amanda: Well, it's not but...

M1: So basically you are mad at her because she told her best friend you broke up with your boyfriend?

Chrissy: Yes. I told her not to tell anybody. That's not right.

M2: It isn't. Did you know your boyfriend cheated on you?

Chrissy: No, I didn't, I just found out right now from you.

M1: Okay. We have to come up with an agreement. You are going to sign it, but if you break it you get in more serious trouble. So you guys have to come up with an agreement.

M2: Are you two planning on being friends afterward?

Chrissy: Listen—I will leave her alone, but I'm not going to trust her no more, or tell her anything. All I'm going to do is stay away from her. That's all I'm going to do. I agree to do that.

M2: If that's what you agree to then that's the way it will be.

M1: Not see each other, just ignore each other?

Amanda: All right, yup, all right.

M1: And please, no name calling in the hallways. Or your friends saying this and that about each other. Whatever goes on in this room, stays in this room.

Chrissy: No doubt.

M1: So you are going to agree not to talk to each other again?

Chrissy: Yeah.

An agreement is written and signed by all parties present.

Mediation 3—Ashley and Simone: Shared Locker

The disputants clarify their sides of the problem privately with mediators, and then all parties are brought together. Mediators (M1, M2, and M3) introduce themselves and explain the rules.

M1: There's no talking to each other. You have to talk to us. There's no cursing. No name calling.

M2: Don't throw anything. Keep your shoes on.

M3: And we don't take sides. Do you want to go first?

Ashley: I'll go. My name is Ashley and me and Simone share a locker since the beginning of school, and she dirtied my coat.

M1: Okay, so you guys are saying that you shared a locker for a long time, and she dirtied it. And you're saying, she is messy or something? She doesn't know how to take care of stuff.

Ashley: Yeah.

Simone: Well, if you knew I was messy, then why did you let me share a locker with you in the first place?

Ashley: Because you're my friend.

Simone: Why are you saying something now?

M1: You have to talk to us.

Simone: All right, when school started, she said we could share a locker. She knew I was messy. I am not going to say I am the neatest person, so why did she wait until now to say something?

M1: Do you have anything to say about that?

Ashley: I don't care if she is messy with her stuff. When it comes to my coat, and my books, that annoys me.

M1: Well, we have to think of some kind of agreement for you to agree on and so this doesn't happen again.

Ashley: She should use her own locker.

M1: Okay. Do you agree on that?

Simone: Fine.

M2: So Simone, you are going to use your own locker now?

Simone: Yeah. Since this is a problem, I can't use her locker.

M1: Okay, so this isn't going to have an effect on your friendship or anything?

Ashley: No.

Simone: No.

M1: All right. I am just writing down what you guys agreed. You guys agreed to not share lockers any more.

M2: And still remain friends?

M1: That's about it or do you guys have anything else to say?

Ashley: That's it.

An agreement is written and all parties sign.

SAC Student Interviews

It would be nice to believe that all mediations end amicably, but that is not always possible. What can be achieved, for those who wish to keep their problem from escalating or to avoid serious disciplinary consequences, is that the heat of the dispute and the threat of actualized violence will be quelled enough for students to return to class and continue on with their academic day.

The reality is that most disputing parties will not "be themselves" that day, affecting how well they may function in class. This is when staff communication becomes so crucial. If the classroom teacher can be made aware of the possibility that the student may be having a difficult time and be kept apprised of the situation, the teacher will be less resentful of time "lost" to the SAC and can help facilitate the student's successful return to normalcy.

To determine the effectiveness of the SAC, some students who have made use of SAC services were asked to complete a questionnaire and, with the benefit of hindsight, agreed to discuss their SAC experiences on tape with teacher and co-author Mary Meggie.

Their transcribed interviews illuminate the range of complex, interrelated problems that arise from dysfunctional home situations and absentee parenting. Problems with drug and alcohol use, relationships, self-esteem issues, feelings of alienation, gang activity, and physical and verbal abuse by parents or step-parents are common themes that are woven throughout their painful, candid reflections shared here in their own words.

Interview 1—Darrell

Darrell is an 18-year-old special education senior whose first love is football. He has a history of confrontational behavior, which has tapered off in recent years. He regularly sees an SAC counselor for one-to-one counseling.

Darrell's brother just returned from prison. His father and step-father are verbally and, occasionally, physically abusive alcoholics. This fall Darrell's sister died of cancer, and now his mother is battling the disease, as well. Darrell's issues are complex and interrelated. With the help of a strong mother and regular counseling and support services from the SAC, Darrell perseveres.

Ms. Meggie: How did the SAC help out, Darrell?

Darrell: A lot of people knew what I was going through. I mean, Mr.–, his brother died. He told me things that happened.

Ms. Meggie: Is he a counselor here?

Darrell: Yeah. He told me what I was going to go through, and, "...don't think that you weren't a good brother..." you know, and they did help me out a lot. They told me what I would be feeling and what was going to happen. And so I was ready for it.

Ms. Meggie: So it just kind of made you feel better to be able to talk with someone who understood?

Darrell: Yeah. And my alcoholic father threatens to kill me.

Ms. Meggie: Are you still living with him?

Darrell: No, I live with my mother. He knew his daughter was dying, and he needed to put pressure on somebody else. My brother was in jail, so he put it on me. He tells me he is going to kill me. My mom said, "He's saying that because he's drunk. He wouldn't hurt you. He's just really mad." I don't talk to him, and I don't want to bring him in my life right now. I want to be stable. He affected my attitude. I was an angry person. I said nothing to nobody. No tolerance. I wasn't being myself. Going to SAC helped me be myself again. I still don't talk to my father.

Ms. Meggie: It still hurts?

Darrell: My brother just got out of jail, and he's hurting too.

Ms. Meggie: Your brother, is he home with you?

Darrell: No, he lives in New Britain.

Ms. Meggie: Your family seems to be all broken up. You get along okay with your mom?

Darrell: Sure. We have our disputes...

Ms. Meggie: Well, everybody does.

Darrell: Like, "Wash the dishes." "I'll do it later Mom," like that. But like any other normal kids.

Ms. Meggie: Your dad, how is he doing with the alcohol?

Darrell: After my sister died I think he drowned himself in it. I think he got really drunk all day. When he drinks he's violent. And he has to find other ways to deal with problems. He hasn't learned to deal with his problems. I have a lot of respect for him as a hard worker, and he keeps his body in good shape, but he disrespects people and their feelings, and he'll say, "Hey, dog," to your face. But behind my back he says I'm a good football player; when they see me on TV running he says, "That's my son." His wife—he got remarried—said he kept every clipping with my name on it. He still wants to be a part of my life, and right now I don't feel like showing him the way; I'm not ready.

Ms. Meggie: Keep a little distance, just to preserve yourself? What made you come to the realization as to what you had to do?

Darrell: When he's in my life...he gives me money because I am his son, he does this for me, but he also gives me a hard time. He wants to run things for me. He wants me to become a man of his stature...I feel that for me to have a good relationship with him, I have to become a man my way. I want to go to college, do my things, then maybe have a relationship. Because right now he wants to teach me how to be a man, you know, in his eyes.

Ms. Meggie: In his way. He wants you to be his idea of a man, not your idea of what a man is.

Darrell: Right. Exactly. When he picks me up, you know, "You got to do this and you should do that." Mostly it is good advice, but you don't pressure me into doing something. And he wasn't there for me. He wasn't there for my brother. My sister told me Trevor waited hours, and he never picked him up. He wanted to do his own thing, and he hurt his kids. He hurt Trevor's feelings.

Ms. Meggie: That's your brother? The one that just got home?

Darrell: Yeah. He could have been a better man, but because of the disappointment of my father, you know, that hurt him. That affected his life. He became an angry person.

Ms. Meggie: What was he arrested for?

Darrell: Ah, probably drugs. I don't do drugs. My mother did not tell me about my father, that he was an alcoholic. I found out mostly from my grandmother. But I found out he did drugs by myself. He does it in my face and tells me not to do it, but how can I respect somebody that does it? I didn't respect him as a man. I know a real man doesn't do that.

Ms. Meggie: Where do you get your guidance, then?

Darrell: My mother. She's been everything. She's been the strongest person in the world, and I put her through a lot of stuff. That's why I respect her, and I will always cherish her. I've seen mean mothers that let their kids do anything and give up on their kids. Kids do alcohol and drugs and stuff. She never had to worry about me doing drugs. 'Cause she knows I wouldn't do it.

Ms. Meggie: You come to the SAC, and what do you get from the SAC? Or do you bring something to the SAC? You kind of have an interesting background because you have so much going on in a negative way that helps you develop in a positive way.

Darrell: My mother always told me to stay positive; when I was playing football—I was really good, but my sister was dying and I didn't go to practice. They took me from the starting lineup and didn't put me back. Last year I made All Conference. I was close to making All State. So this year, not playing at all, I was frustrated. I wanted to quit. And my mother said, "Stick it out. Do it out for you, not me." I was going to quit something I loved. She hates football, but she would not let me quit 'cause she knows I was good at it, and I could do something with it...

Ms. Meggie: Do you come here much for fighting?

Darrell: (pause) No.

Ms. Meggie: So you just needed the SAC as a cooling-off place?

Darrell: It's a cooling off place, but like I said, I talked to Mr.—. He helped me realize what's going to happen.

Ms. Meggie: Coping with death and change in life.

Darrell: Yeah. Exactly. Sometimes I need advice from other people. You know. It was like, "What's out there that can really benefit me?" That's when the SAC helped.

Ms. Meggie: You're keeping clean? No drugs, no alcohol.

Darrell: No drugs, no alcohol.

Ms. Meggie: You just got to watch your fist?

Darrell: Yeah, all the men in my family got to watch that. My father has a low tolerance, but my brother's tolerance is zero.

Ms. Meggie: But do you just go off, when you're *not* provoked? I mean, it seems like you've been pushed pretty badly for you to strike back. But it doesn't seem like you go off on your own.

Darrell: No, maybe in the past, but as I've grown, I don't provoke fights. I just walk away...Like, the beginning of the year I walked away from somebody, and he hit me. And it was all caught on camera. I got arrested and they wrote the story in the paper, and it said I was released on a $1,000 bond. The paper wrote like we were going at it, but that's not what happened...I got on a bus and this guy had his leg out, and I accidentally hit it. I said, "My bad," and he started talking trash. I got up and I forget it and I turned my back. He said, "I hit you. Don't mess with me 'cause I hit you." I go, "My bad" and turned my back, and he hit me. I grabbed him, and threw him over a couple of seats.

Ms. Meggie: Is this a school bus or regular bus?

Darrell: School bus. It was caught on tape.

Ms. Meggie: Ten days [out of school]?

Darrell: Five days. He got ten days.

As we wrapped up our conversation, it was clear that Darrell recognized that he had come a long way, and he was pleased with his progress and optimistic about the future.

Interview 2—Amber

Amber is a precocious 14-year-old who has been cutting herself regularly and has been physically abusive to her mother. Her ready smile and earnest eyes belie the anguish she feels.

As with many others, it was a peer referral that brought her to the SAC. Amber confided to a friend that she has been cutting her wrists. The concerned friend contacted the SAC director who paired Amber with a social work college intern to whom she could relate. They established a trusting relationship in their ongoing one-to-one sessions, where the emphasis is on helping Amber deal with her many anger issues.

Amber's situation illustrates the breadth of the problems many of our "urban orphans" face, with parents more consumed with their own issues than their child's. For Amber the SAC fills a void. What brings Amber back to work on her problems is the level of trust established in the SAC. It is a place to belong.

Ms. Meggie: Okay, Amber, you said your friends recommended that you come to the SAC? You have been slashing at your wrist with a knife; you had done it before, and you said, pretty much, you have done it because...?

Amber: Well, anger. From everything. Daily.

Ms. Meggie: Daily anger. And your dad is in rehab?

Amber: Uhum. In and out of my life.

Ms. Meggie: Your parents never married? You said something about your step-father, there was some anger...?

Amber: Yeah, he tries too much to be my father and I don't like that. He's twenty-seven! And he's acting like a kid himself. He makes fun of me, he'll do childish stuff, and I'm more of an adult than he is. But I don't say shit when he says stuff, like if he says, "You little brat," I'll say bad stuff back because it just annoys me. "You're my mom's boyfriend. You don't have a right to say stuff like that to me." I put up with it because I want my mom to be happy, but deep down inside I am hurting. You know. I had my mother to myself since I was a baby, and then she just starting dating him five years ago. So it was, like, I can't have my mom to myself anymore. She doesn't care as long as she has what she wants. I don't have what I want. I don't want my mom's boyfriend as my father. I basically think he took my mom away from me. People say, "No he didn't," But I don't feel that way, you know?

Ms. Meggie: Do you have brothers and sisters?

Amber: I have a half-brother and I haven't seen him in like nine years and I really, really want to see him. My mom talks to his mother all the time. He's nineteen.

Ms. Meggie: Now, he's your father's son?

Amber: Yeah, and I call him my brother. You know, we talk on the phone, like, a while ago, and I sent him a Christmas card, and we are trying to keep in touch, but he's old–he's 18 and he wants to be with his friends and stuff like that. My father doesn't want us to see each other, but I tell him I'm going to see Barry.

Ms. Meggie: Why does he not want you to see him?

Amber: He is afraid we are going to talk. My mom is good friends with his mom, and he's afraid we're going to talk about him, and we're going to go to court because my father hasn't paid child support–he has paid like five child supports in ten years.

Ms. Meggie: So, pretty much, his life has been in rehab?

Amber: Yeah, in rehab and going from job to job. He has a certificate saying he can do brick laying for the union and stuff.

Ms. Meggie: That pays well.

Amber: Yeah, but he ruins it because he has a temper himself and he does stuff. He hits them or he fights with them. Or they will find out, like, he lied on his application for a job and fire him...He has gotten arrested before. He's stole stuff. He'd done a lot of stuff, basically, so that can get him in trouble. You know?

Ms. Meggie: He has a temper, too? You have a temper?

Amber: Yes, I take after my father a lot. Like when I'm angry I'll hit. Like if my mom pushes me, that kind of thing, I'll hit her back, because I just get so angry. People say it's because of the way I was brought up, around fighting, and that's me. People say, you know, what goes on in your childhood is what you carry on. I can see that happening, because my father used to hit my mother, and I take after my father in a lot of ways. I think I am starting to take after him because of my temper. It gets to a point where I can't take it any more. And if I don't hit something, I am going to cut myself, you know? I haven't cut myself in, like, three weeks.

Ms. Meggie: And how often do you cut yourself?

Amber: Once or twice a week. And I do it in the same spot to open it up.

Ms. Meggie: You just take a razor?

Amber: I never had a razor. I used to make noise going downstairs to get a knife, so I couldn't do that. So I take scissors that are new and sharp. And it does not hurt me. I don't feel pain when I cut myself. That's why I keep doing it and doing it until I think I feel pain, you know? It's like the pain I feel here, it bleeds because it's the pain that I feel in here, going all out right there.

Ms. Meggie: So you feel better after?

Amber: Yeah, umhum.

Ms. Meggie: What made you come to the SAC? Your friend urged you to come and then you met Miss–, one of our interns?

Amber: Yeah. It helped me a lot. I talk to her about my boyfriend and a lot about stuff that happened to me. Not before I had my boyfriend, and that's a whole different story, and she helped me get through it.

Ms. Meggie: How did she–by talking?

Amber: Yeah. She's been through it, you know? And she's real cool when it comes to stuff like that. I know she would not say a word about anything. I guess there is stuff, I guess you could say she was probably recommended to tell somebody, but she just knew that if she helped me through it then it will be okay.

Ms. Meggie: So then you see that there's progress and it's been three weeks and you haven't done anything, even though you had that experience where your dad took off on you on New Years?

Amber: Uhum. There's so much I could have cut myself about in the last three weeks, and I just sat in my bed and cried. I didn't want to cut myself because I promised my boyfriend, I promised my cousin, because she did it, too. I told her, "Cara, this is what I've been doing," and she said, "I've been doing it, too." And it's weird because our problems are similar. I'm not saying I'm worse because there's no comparing somebody's problems. You know?

Ms. Meggie: Yes. That's a very mature thing to recognize.

Amber: Yes, I know her problems are not worse or better than mine. We talk about our problems, and she hasn't done it for a while which made me think, why am I still doing it? I should stop, you know? And she's given me strength, too. I need support because if I'm left by myself, there is no way I am going to get through everything. And I feel I'm getting it here.

Ms. Meggie: Why come here instead of to the guidance office?

Amber: I don't know, these are more friendly people. I don't have to worry, I can trust them. Guidance, I went there in middle school, and it didn't get me anywhere. All they do is talk to you about your problems. They didn't help you with your problems. They just kind of listen to you. But I'd rather have someone give you advice, and this is what they do. They give you advice, and they help you through it. If you are having a problem and you don't want to go to the next class because that person's in there, they will let you stay, you know not *every day*. But then they will take the person in here, and they'll talk with the person and you...

Ms. Meggie: It seems like you kept away from drugs and stuff like that. Maybe you've seen it with your father.

Amber: Yeah. I don't want to end up like that. I'm not being like my father. I have my father's temper, but you can easily overcome that. You can't easily overcome alcohol and drugs.

Ms. Meggie: It seems like you are coming to terms with the fact that your father has serious problems.

Amber: Uhha. And I can't help him.

Ms. Meggie: No, you can't. But you have a really good handle on yourself. It sounds like you would make a good counselor.

Amber: Yeah, that's what I want to be.

Ms. Meggie: I think you would be very good at it.

Interview 3—Jamie

Jamie is a mature, sensitive 15-year-old sophomore who works in the SAC one period a day as a peer mediator. She came to the SAC with a problem commonly addressed in the SAC, betrayed trust. Jamie appreciates the private, confidential environment in which personal problems are aired.

Jamie discusses the peer mediation process and her own involvement with a disputant who "just refused to settle things." Her experience illustrates that not everyone is willing to make peace. But at least the mediation helped prevent the problem from escalating, even though the friendship could not be repaired.

Ms. Meggie: So what do you do in the SAC, Jamie?

Jamie: Usually in the morning I come up here and I do whatever they have me do, and I just do peer mediations.

Ms. Meggie: So you have been trained in the peer mediation process? How did you like that?

Jamie: It was interesting.

Ms. Meggie: How do you handle peer mediation?

Jamie: Um, we have the disputants sit in a different area just in case there's a strong, really big argument that might result in a fight. We separate them, and we tell them the rules, which is one person talks at a time; talk directly to the peer mediator instead of at each other; no swearing; and while one person's telling their story, you can't say anything or interrupt. We hear both sides of the story, and repeat back the story. Then we explain what can be done to help the situation out and help them come to an agreement. You know, to say how they plan to make things better instead of going into a fight.

Ms. Meggie: Do you talk among yourselves without the others hearing you? Do the mediators talk without the disputants? Or are you always together to discuss things in front of each other?

Jamie: We usually discuss things in front of each other. During mediation we don't really talk to each other. We listen to the stories, and that's when everyone talks, in one big group, to solve the problem.

Ms. Meggie: You said you actually came here and used the process yourself. What happened?

Jamie: I believe that was last year, my freshman year.

Ms. Meggie: Do you want to tell me what happened? There was a big commotion, you had said.

Jamie: Yeah, between me and a friend of mine. We were friends, but not any more. She is related to me. She is my cousin, but we thought of each other as best friends. We met in the 8th grade and became really good friends throughout the year. Before 8th grade graduation, we found out we were related. So that kind of got us closer together. And we spent the whole summer together. Then 9th grade started and things just changed. Usually when you come to high school you change a little because you're in a bigger school, bigger people and all. I really don't know what happened, but there was a situation with another friend of ours. She told me a secret and somehow it got around, and they blamed it on me. So then my cousin got in it and started saying bad stuff about me.

Ms. Meggie: She thought you had told the secret as well?

Jamie: Umhum. They all blamed me. And then she went and told a bunch of stories to get them all mad at me, which worked. When I straightened it out, I didn't get to straighten out anything with her because she wouldn't really talk to me or anything. She thought I tried to get everyone mad at her, which is not what happened. So throughout the rest of the year we never really talked.

Ms. Meggie: You are missing the friendship, I bet?

Jamie: Yeah. And usually if we look at each other we give each other dirty looks. And she is always talking about me. At the beginning of the year she brought me up here. She said, "Oh, I heard you were talking junk, whatever," and I was like, "No, I heard you were talking junk..."

Ms. Meggie: So what kind of things is she saying?

Jamie: During last year the incident—she would say that I was talking junk about this girl's brother, and I said that this girl—I don't want to say the word.

Ms. Meggie: A whore?

Jamie: Yeah. I didn't want to say the word. She said that I called her that, and they got really mad and brought me up here.

Ms. Meggie: And you never said that?

Jamie: I never said that.

Ms. Meggie: But the other girl brought you up, too? Because she thought you said it about her?

Jamie: Yeah. The two girls that heard that from my cousin brought me up here. We settled it and everything. But the little differences between me and my cousin, it wouldn't work because she refused to settle things.

Ms. Meggie: Well, how did the mediation result? What happened after you came up here?

Jamie: They said obviously someone was saying something that wasn't true. My friends believed my side of the story, because they knew I wouldn't do that. They've seen the good side of me and they've seen the bad, which really isn't bad. So they knew I was telling the truth. When it was time to settle it, my cousin just didn't cooperate at all. She said, "Oh you did say this and you did say that," and I was like, "No, I didn't say anything! You're saying all this stuff, trying to get people to turn their backs on me, when it really shouldn't go that way." So for Christmas, New Years, any holiday, I don't want to spend it with her. Her parents came over my house a few days ago, and they had Christmas gifts for us. Only her brother came, her and her sister did not come.

Ms. Meggie: Do you miss her still as a friend?

Jamie: I kind of do, but then it's like I wish I never met her.

Ms. Meggie: So this was a good experience with the SAC, that you wanted to come back, or did you come back for another problem or another point?

Jamie: I don't know. I did come up for other problems, but they weren't as serious. Kids like to come up here to keep it in a closed environment without letting anybody else know. If you talk it out in the hallway and you raise your voices, everyone thinks that a fight is going to go on, so people get nosy. That's why people come here; they like to keep it confidential and everything.

Ms. Meggie: Keep it private. So when you left the SAC that day knowing that your cousin probably wasn't going to change her mind, how did you feel when you left? Do you remember?

Jamie: I really didn't feel relieved because she wouldn't cooperate at all. So I really didn't know what she was thinking.

Ms. Meggie: How were you able to put a distance on it? And feel, "All right, it didn't work, but I can put a distance on it?"

Jamie: Well, the fact that she still would go and talk behind my back with my friends, and I kind of figured it out—I knew she was talking junk about me, and it wasn't even worth it to talk to her. She is not even going to compromise.

Ms. Meggie: But obviously you are able to walk away from it and hold your head up and not let it affect the way you feel about people. Have you found a good friend to fill her place?

Jamie: Actually, yeah.

Ms. Meggie: That helps, doesn't it?

Jamie: Umhum. It hurts, though, to lose a good friend.

Ms. Meggie: Yeah; that happens to be a relative, too. It's hard. Well, she's losing too, right? It sounds like she lost a good friend in you. Well, so you like the mediation process and you like being a mediator? What is it you like best about it?

Jamie: I like to help people. My aunt calls me "advice woman" or something. People ask me everything, and I give them advice out of nowhere, and it actually works. A friend said, "You should be a peer mediator. You could help people out." I never thought about that—and it was actually good. I talked to Mr. Gwozdz and...

Ms. Meggie: And it's working for you. You've been very helpful for the department.

Jamie smiled with pride, replacing the gentle sadness that had crept into her voice as she mourned the lost friendship. She had found a place in the SAC where her contributions were valued.

Interview 4—Luisa

Luisa is a poised, soft-spoken senior who just turned nineteen. She arrived in East Hartford from Puerto Rico as a freshman, and like so many of our new students, her limited fluency in English set her apart and created some adjustment problems for her. She was being teased and made fun of because of this. Upon referral from her assistant principal, Luisa was teamed with a bilingual counselor as well as a peer mediator to work through her difficulties, particularly with her peers. Here she explains her SAC experience in her vastly improved English.

Ms. Meggie: So you have been coming here for four years, and you have been having good results.

Luisa: Yeah. I came here because I needed help with personal problems and stuff. When I was a freshman it was because the girl's having problems with me. My principal sent me here to fix it. They was making fun of me because I didn't know English; they were talking about me in English. My cousin told me they were talking about me. That's how I found out.

Ms. Meggie: And it hurt your feelings?

Luisa: Yeah it hurt me a lot 'cause I thought it was my friends, you know, and that really hurt me. And they bring up to argument, and they bring us to security guard, and my assistant principal decided to bring us here. By that time Mr.– was here.

Ms. Meggie: Oh, Mr.–. Yeah, he's nice.

Luisa: Yeah, and he speaks English and Spanish.

Ms. Meggie: And what happened? How did it all work out? You came up here. You saw Mr.–.

Luisa: Yeah, and Mr. Gwozdz, they give me peer mediator.

Ms. Meggie: A peer mediator. Did they know Spanish, too.

Luisa: Ahha. So we went. It was really cool. Then we finish. After that we talk, but not like before, the people with problems with me. We was talking but it wasn't the same. It was really cool.

Ms. Meggie: Well, it was not the same how? Better? Worse?

Luisa: It seemed better.

Ms. Meggie: What did they say?

Luisa: "Well, we was talking about you 'cause you quiet, you different." And I said, "Well, you got to understand that I come from another country. I don't know nobody, so you just give me some time and I probably get to know you guys better. I can learn more English if you guys help me. You guys not helping me talking about me." And after that they actually help me.

Ms. Meggie: Were they whispering? Did they make up stuff?

Luisa: It was just making stories up and just whispering like.

Ms. Meggie: They are talking about, like, what you're wearing?

Luisa: Aha. Yeah. They was talking about that. They actually admit that here. They was talking about the way I was dressing, my hair, the way that I look.

Ms. Meggie: So all things that were superficial.

Luisa: Yeah.

Ms. Meggie: They realized what they were doing was mean?

Luisa: They actually realize.

Ms. Meggie: The peer mediator made them realize this? And they stopped the whispering?

Luisa: Yeah, they actually start helping me with me homework and everything.

Ms. Meggie: Now, you were a freshman when you first came here. Now you're in grade 12.

Luisa: Yeah.

Ms. Meggie: Have you been here for any other reasons?

Luisa: When I was a sophomore, my friend was with me, and he was going out with a freshman and the freshman thought I was going out with him. Like back and forth, and I say bad stuff, and I just gonna bring them to SAC. They help. We got peer mediator and that girl that I was trying to talk to, she don't know English so I ask Mr.– to come over here and he help me. It was kind of cool, and after that, I help her with the English. In the junior year I came over here to start my problems, my personal problems. My parents are having problem. And that affected me because I not there with them. They live in Puerto Rico, but sometime they call me and talk about problems, and that they worry about me, you know.

Ms. Meggie: You were hearing your parents' problems on the telephone?

Luisa: Yeah, and I came over here and Mrs.– [a social worker], she's here, and I start going to group with Ms.– [an intern]. And she help me. She help me a lot.

Ms. Meggie: Now, how come you prefer to go to her rather than your counselor downstairs?

Luisa: Because she talks to me like real. She talks to me the way I need someone to talk to. My counselor, they not the same. They tell me "yeah" if it works for me. They talk to me and stuff, but not the way she talks to me–like real, you know? I don't know how to say it. She's really open. She makes me feel good the way she talks to me. She talks more my language. She don't speak Spanish, but the way she talks to me, it was good. I came over here this year too because of personal problems, but she's not here now so it was kind of hard for me to find somebody up here.

Ms. Meggie: Is there somebody up here that you can talk to that's pretty good? Another intern?

Luisa: Yeah. Mr.–. He really helps me a lot.

Ms. Meggie: So your problems still deal with your family?

Luisa: Yeah–family, friends. Sometimes I get depressed and stuff, so I just talk to him. At first I was shy, and he was the only one that noticed it, like "Something's wrong with you," and I was like, "If he noticed it then I probably should talk to him." But it will take time, like two months to let it out.

Ms. Meggie: You mean open up with him?

Luisa: Yeah. Right now I think, thanks to him I am here now.

Ms. Meggie: Really.

Luisa: Yeah, 'cause there's a lot of stuff going on.

Ms. Meggie: You weren't thinking of killing yourself were you?

Luisa: Um.

Ms. Meggie: Yeah? You were feeling pretty low? Was it missing your family?

Luisa: Missing my family. Problems in school. It stress me out and stuff, my job.

Ms. Meggie: Too much school work?

Luisa: Yeah. But right now I feel good. Right now I'm on the top. I'm not taking it really hard. And they help me a lot. When I have problems, I know I can come over here and talk to them. I can even talk to Mr. Gwozdz and he can talk to me. And it stay over here. It don't go around. I can count on them.

Ms. Meggie: Does it have to do with your parents? Do you think they're getting divorced?

Luisa: No, they actually got married. The problem is that my father kind of drinks.

Ms. Meggie: Ah. And you can't deal with that?

Luisa: No. But he's getting help now. He wants to come here, but I don't want to live with him. I want to stay with my aunt.

Ms. Meggie: She doesn't have any alcohol problems she's dealing with, and you don't need to see alcohol problems.

Luisa: No. My mom was always there, but not like the stuff I been through here, school, the new language. My aunt has been there for me, and help me a lot...But right now I feel really good.

Ms. Meggie: Your depression is getting better?

Luisa: Yeah. A lot better.

Ms. Meggie: You have friends.

Luisa: Yeah, I have more friends—everywhere I go it's like, "Hi Luisa." I have a lot of friends now.

Ms. Meggie: So you recommend the SAC to other people?

Luisa: I do, because SAC—when you need help, but not only when you need help—when you need to talk to somebody or you feel lonely, SAC is the place. SAC helps in everything: class problems, personal problems, everything. Especially when you have a fight with somebody, and you don't want to get suspended or you don't want to fight, just come to the SAC and they help you.

Ms. Meggie: Do you ever feel like you want to fight?

Luisa: Not me. When I was a freshman here, yeah, but not now. I changed a lot. They help me a lot. Like the peer mediator, they talk to me and they say, "You should do this." I don't want to fight. I don't even want to get in an argument with that person. So I just bring the person over here, and I get one of the peer mediators, and they help me. And I get out of the room with the person, talking with the person, friends, you know?

Ms. Meggie: Like the way you wanted it to be before?

Luisa: Yeah, and SAC help me a lot. I recommend this place to a lot of people. Like the people, they be scared to talk to anybody. These people are good. They kind of like family. That's the way that I put it, like family. Because they really good. They help.

Interview 5—Tanya

Many issues dealt with through the SAC originate outside of school. Problems with dating, relationships, and he-said, she-said disputes that wear down students' abilities to focus on academics.

Tanya is a 16-year-old junior from a low-income housing project which is often a hotbed for rumors, arguments, and violence. As a freshman, she came to the SAC to resolve a problem with her boyfriend and, later, to squelch an escalating group dispute. To head off an all-out brawl and mass suspensions, the disputants were brought together to resolve the problem. Tanya describes how these situations were mediated.

Ms. Meggie: Tanya, how did you find out about the SAC?

Tanya: By a friend of mine, because I was having problems with my boyfriend. She recommended me to come over here.

Ms. Meggie: Tell me what happened with your boyfriend?

Tanya: Basically some problems, and I ended up going off on him in the hallway. So I had to come here.

Ms. Meggie: Oh. What did you do?

Tanya: I kind of hit him.

Ms. Meggie: Did he say something about you? What happened?

Tanya: Well, we was together about one year and then another friend told me that he was messing with another female, and they was sexually active. So I went back to the girl, and she said yeah, they was talking, but she didn't know he was with me. So when he came into the school I couldn't hold back. And when I asked him, he just looked at me and I got so nervous I hit him.

Ms. Meggie: And so he had been sleeping with her?

Tanya: Yeah. But not that long. I think it was just once. And he said it just happened.

Ms. Meggie: Um. Were you sleeping with him too?

Tanya: Yeah. And he was my first and my only.

Ms. Meggie: And was he using protection?

Tanya: I don't know if he was with her, but I know I was.

Ms. Meggie: He used a condom? Or you used birth control?

Tanya: Oh, condom.

Ms. Meggie: So at least, you know, for purposes of disease...

Tanya: Yes.

Ms. Meggie: It is one thing to feel someone cheated on you, but...So you swung at him?

Tanya: I swung at him, but I couldn't reach. So I kind of just grabbed my purse, which had a heavy mirror in it which I forgot about, and I hit him against the head with it. And he bent down, and I kept hitting him and then I walked away angry.

Ms. Meggie: So what happened? Did someone bring you here, that day when you swung at him?

Tanya: Yeah. A security guard did. They just brought me up here, and we just talked for a good hour.

Ms. Meggie: Describe how that was handled.

Tanya: Actually, two of the counselors sat in the room and then, I didn't want to say anything in front of them, and he stood quiet on the other side of the room. It was like they were going to leave us alone, but I wasn't allowed to hit him or anything. They basically left and I just talked to him. Yelling, but talking to him.

Ms. Meggie: Now did you have a mediator with you?

Tanya: At first, but then I didn't want to say anything in front of them so they just left.

Ms. Meggie: You thought it was too personal?

Tanya: Yeah. So they decided to leave, and we stood in the room by ourselves.

Ms. Meggie: Now, that was when you were a freshman, and now you are a junior. And older and wiser... How are things? How has the SAC served a purpose for you over the years?

Tanya: It's a pretty good situation because whenever I'm having—like when something happens, I can always come over here, don't have to worry about being stressed out in class. Or having to skip a class because I really don't want to go to that class, because I'm stressed out.

Ms. Meggie: Does that really help when you get upset?

Tanya: Oh, yes. Umhum. Very much.

Ms. Meggie: Can't focus and...

Tanya: Yeah. I can't at all because I keep thinking about it.

Ms. Meggie: You can't get it out your head. Now, it says here that you came here with problems with other people. You talked about this fight with a girlfriend?

Tanya: My best friend. She was next to my locker, and this girl starting yelling at my friend. My friend isn't allowed to fight 'cause she's on probation for another fight, her first fight. So I didn't want her to fight but the girl jumped on her and started hitting her. I grabbed the girl, but she was tall—I didn't reach her, so I pulled her by the hair to get her off, and it ended up becoming this huge conflict. When we got here, we was supposed to get suspended for ten days, but they decided if we all got together with the mediators we wouldn't get suspended. That worked out.

Ms. Meggie: So what happened with the peer mediators? Why did this other girl want to fight your friend?

Tanya: Oh, she was walking past us, and she had got new sneakers and my friend says, "Oh, they look cute," but she misunderstood and thought it was that her outfit didn't match her sneakers. So she started going off for no reason. Then even after we agree with the counselor, like, nobody listened. The next day a girl that had nothing to do with it got involved. All the girls just wanted to go and roll and stuff, and it became this huge conflict.

Ms. Meggie: So you mean the fight continued on the next day?

Tanya: It wasn't a fight; it was just yelling and threatening.

Ms. Meggie: And where was that done? This was after school?

Tanya: Umhum. And in the morning, in my projects where I live. All my friends had to watch to make sure those girls weren't coming because we all live in the projects, and we always got to be watching our backs. Mr. Gwozdz says once you got a problem, just forget about them and ignore them in school. But it's different; you see these people every day, so you have to either resolve it now, or then you are just going to get into this huge fight.

Ms. Meggie: How do you feel the school helped or didn't help?

Tanya: It did help because if we didn't get it resolved here in school while all these teachers are here and stuff, then it would have become this huge fight between ten girls, where we could have all got arrested. And somebody could have got hurt.

Ms. Meggie: But the fight was defused then? Did you get a peer mediator here that day?

Tanya: Yeah, I forget her name. There's the two mediators. They is here now, and Mr. Gwozdz himself.

Ms. Meggie: And what was the decision on the second day? What were some of the choices of how to handle your differences?

Tanya: Basically that we just couldn't say anything to each other. If we did, we get suspended. I don't want to get suspended. I never got suspended and if I do it's gonna mess up my record. So I came back here, and they put us all in the meeting room downstairs with Dr. Edwards, and we all said what happened.

Ms. Meggie: The mediators were downstairs with you?

Tanya: Yeah.

Ms. Meggie: And what did the mediators do during all this?

Tanya: They kind of sat there and kind of heard us, what we were saying to each other, and said, "Yeah that's what happened the first day when they came up." And it all ended up that this one girl started the whole rumor, and she wasn't even there. So it just ended up her friends turned their back on her. And it was, "So you started this and it had nothing to do with us."

Ms. Meggie: Could you say pretty much that it was ended after the second mediation?

Tanya: Yeah. Basically.

Ms. Meggie: Yeah. So pretty much SAC has worked for you?

Tanya: Oh, yeah.

Ms. Meggie: Would you recommend it to other kids?

Tanya: Yeah. You could resolve a lot of fights coming in here.

Ms. Meggie: What kind of people would you suggest use the SAC, or for what reason?

Tanya: Basically anything. Arguments that you have with somebody. Any kind of rumors you hear, because I know especially if you coming from an urban area you got to be respected. So if you talking about me I'm gonna come up to you, and if that other person's not going to let you disrespect them, it's gonna end up becoming this huge fight. And I know this way, this is working real good. I would recommend this to other people.

Interview 6—Jason

Some students directed to the Student Assistance Center become valuable human assets to the peer mediation process, as is true with Jason, one of the SAC's successful mediators.

Jason is a shy, well-mannered sophomore who was referred to the SAC by a teacher who was disturbed by the drawing of machine guns with which he bordered his failing math test. The teacher thought this might be some sort of threat and contacted the SAC social worker, also concerned that he might be suicidal.

As it turned out, Jason was having difficulty transitioning from middle school to high school. His grades were slipping and his self-described "demented" sense of humor caused some of his teachers and classmates to view him as "weird."

Jason sought short-term private counseling on his own, which was reinforced by on-going support from the SAC social worker. In the process, Jason's self-esteem began to rise. He proved himself to be a responsible worker and a good listener—an excellent mediator. It is the active listening skills that Jason acquired during his peer mediation training that he feels are most valuable to both his social and academic future, as this interview illustrates.

Ms. Meggie: So how did you come to be a peer mediator?

Jason: They found need for me, I guess. They found out I was an excellent worker, and they were constantly commenting to me on what a great job I did around here. So I figured this is pretty cool—I guess I will just stay here instead of sitting around in study hall. It's better that I get to talk to people here that I know.

Ms. Meggie: And these people respect you. They say that you are an excellent mediator.

Jason: I've done maybe three or four mediations—I'm still kind of new to them. The ones that I have done are—well, better than the regular mediators, let's say. First I worked with other mediators so that I could see what happens in a normal mediation and learn from it.

Ms. Meggie: And what did you like about the whole process?

Jason: It's excellent.

Ms. Meggie: What is it that you were able to find out about yourself as a mediator? Or why you were good at it? Had to be a strength that came out?

Jason: I guess it is just that I listen a lot more than I talk. So when I listen, I think what is going on; I think through it to find a possible solution. At every interval that they stop and look to me for an answer or a question, and then I try to think of some way that I can help the two people so that they can just—what is the word?—that they can just compromise.

Ms. Meggie: What is it that you have to do to come up with those solutions? What are you doing that is not a written process?

Jason: Try to keep your ears open for details. If more than one person are mad at each other, try to keep them away from each other. And from fighting, because that is mainly what we are trying to do is keep them from fighting. And try to think of any way to have everyone come to a compromise—something they can all agree on. Some way that they can all get through their day.

Ms. Meggie: All buy into the decision made so they can all agree? That's a very mature thought process. You like doing that?

Jason: Yeah.

Ms. Meggie: What did you learn from the veteran mediators?

Jason: I've picked up some techniques to keep people from getting at each other's throats. Like instead of having them talk directly to each other, try to get both sides of the story. And then you can ask individual questions to each one of them or you have them question each other through you. So you would be sort of like the middleman in there. We try to keep the people from talking directly to each other because after a while sparks will fly and they will start yelling and screaming and probably leap at each other's throats. I've seen it happen a couple of times in groups.

Ms. Meggie: So this is a good technique you picked out from some of the veterans.

Jason: Yeah.

Ms. Meggie: It's a lot to be learned. Anything else?

Jason: Not really, except for a small sense of humor, trying to put it in with the mediations.

Ms. Meggie: Humor works.

Jason: Yeah, as long as it isn't directed at the person, but at something in the past that they found funny. You can sort of direct it at that. They might actually laugh. They might get a little bit mad but...

Ms. Meggie: But humor goes a long way. Maybe humor got you here to begin with.

Jason: Humor got me here to begin with and it's probably going to end up pulling me through a lot of things. It's gotten me into things, but it's also gotten me out of things.

Ms. Meggie: It sounds like you have been a big help to this whole program. Would you recommend it for other kids?

Jason: Definitely. Definitely.

Ms. Meggie: What kind of kids do you think it could benefit the most?

Jason: Probably people who are not feeling too good about themselves. People who are really timid and shy can actually make excellent mediators. Like, I remember I was really timid and shy and I used to blush just talking to someone, but I have come a long way from that.

Ms. Meggie: This is your sophomore year. How are you doing this year academically? How is this commitment working the SAC?

Jason: It is working good because some of my friends sometimes can't really figure something out in class and sometimes, up here in mediations, it can actually help you out with schoolwork. Because you have to have a real good ear for detail in the groups and mediations, so that way you can help them come to an agreement. Which also carries on into when you do classwork and when you're talking, when you're in a conversation or a business interview, because you would need to hear everything that the person says because, that way, you would be able to answer their question fully. Or be able to take notes for an exam.

Ms. Meggie: So you learned to be a really good listener. You learned to pick up on detail. That's terrific. I think you are going to be an excellent mediator. Whatever you choose to do, it seems like you are destined to work with people in some way.

Jason: In some way or another.

Ms. Meggie: Do you have a plan for the future?

Jason: I was probably thinking in the lines of architectural design or electrical engineer.

Ms. Meggie: Really? Those aren't with people too much...

Jason: I figured when I was older, maybe like 57, I figured maybe I could open a small bar somewhere, be a bartender there.

Ms. Meggie: Why not counseling? That doesn't appeal to you?

Jason: No not really, I don't think I would make a good counselor. Because hearing everything day in and day out for years eventually starts to crawl on you, probably.

Chapter 5

Other Elements of the SAC
How to Make Your Program
Fit Your Community

Violence Prevention Groups

Drug and Alcohol Abuse Programs

Cultural Enrichment Programs

Career Beginnings

Other Programs

69

This chapter examines the different programs that make up the Student Assistance Center at East Hartford High School and offers suggestions for starting new, unique programs in other communities. In developing your SAC, pay attention to your initial survey results and to any emerging needs.

Violence Prevention Groups

Violence prevention ensures our schools are non-threatening and provide an emotionally and socially stable environment. The key lies in prevention—providing our youth with avenues for airing disputes and socially acceptable alternatives and tools for heading off physical confrontations.

One such vehicle is a violence prevention group. Students who have been involved in fights are targeted to participate in a six-week-long "insight" program that focuses on what happens during a fight and offers techniques kids can use for anger management.

The team itself is comprised of small groups of students who have been suspended for fighting. They meet once a week for six weeks to focus on healthy ways to work out problems or differences. In an intimate, non-threatening environment, students who were suspended from school for fighting can return to school with a transitional support mechanism in place. Here they can discuss the evolution of their hostilities, and eventually both understand and implement alternative methods to resolve problems.

A relevant curriculum should be created—one that emphasizes choices, such as mediation, one that helps students generate new options to be used to resolve conflicts before they escalate to the physical, a curriculum similar to that proposed by Deborah Prothrow-Stith, M.D., from Harvard University, who created the *Violence Prevention Curriculum for Adolescents* (1987).

Drug and Alcohol Abuse Programs

East Hartford High School confronted the substance-abuse problem and its assorted issues early on. Recognizing the scope of the dropout rate and the drug-use problem, administrators applied for and got a grant to fund a specialist in the field.

When trying to start a drug and alcohol program, it is necessary to gain the services of a professional drug and alcohol counselor. Groups like Alateen and Alcoholics Anonymous (AA) can then be contacted and programs developed within the school.

Drug and alcohol programs provide both group and individual counseling to those students who abuse drugs and/or alcohol or who have family members who do. In addition to the Alateen and Alcoholics Anonymous meetings held in school, two types of introductory groups should be held by a certified drug and alcohol counselor.

The first is for concerned persons who have a family member or friend who suffers from an addiction. This functions as a support group, focusing on coping skills and providing support, validation, empathy, and a sympathetic ear. While they meet all year long, membership in Alateen is also encouraged.

The second group is a mandatory drug and alcohol "insight" program for students who have violated drug and alcohol policy or have been otherwise referred. This group meets for six weeks. (See Appendix 13.) Once students have completed this program, they are further referred to AA, which meets once a week in the school. This is a standard AA meeting which is assisted by young AA presenters.

Cultural Enrichment Programs

The Cultural Enrichment Programs involve both visiting and hosting cultural center delegates from local colleges or universities. Trips to cultural events as well as on-site, in-school presentations are held each year. Programming in East Hartford tends to concentrate on Hispanic, Asian, and African-American issues. Students help develop ideas and plan events.

Exposure to such programs fosters understanding and respect for individual differences. When instituting cultural enrichment activities, it is important to contact local universities, community agencies, state programs, museums, and historical societies to help develop specific ideas for presentations that suit the community. The rewards of such efforts are highly satisfying in developing ethnic pride and building community spirit and understanding.

Career Beginnings

Instituted in 1995 at East Hartford High School, Career Beginnings is designed to raise the awareness of participating students about their higher education and career options. A Career Beginnings flyer highlights its aim to:

> Link higher education, public schools, businesses, community volunteers and parents in a coordinated effort to increase the percentage of teenagers who graduate from high school, pursue higher education and fulfill career goals. (Bloomfield, 1989)

Career Beginnings targets a well-defined subset of the school's population, one that often times is ignored by special services (Bloomfield, 1989). It outlines the following requirements for eligibility and selection:

1. Current enrollment as a high-school junior, with projected eligibility for graduation by the end of the senior year.

2. Regular school attendance, with no significant history of disciplinary problems in school or in the community.

3. Average academic achievement; that is, falling in the middle 60 percent of their class.

4. Demonstration of personal motivation and commitment

beyond typical school activities, such as participation in some form of community-based service or working part-time to contribute to the family income.

5. At least 50 percent must meet the federal definition of poverty.

6. At least 80 percent must be first-generation higher-education students, that is, come from families in which neither parent has more than a high-school diploma.

Participants are usually first-generation college-bound students. They develop a hands-on awareness of the total college experience, from application to graduation. Students matriculate at institutions ranging from local community colleges and technical schools to nationally known institutions of higher learning.

During the first year, the students selected attend bimonthly meetings. Workshops are held at area colleges addressing topics including community building, self-awareness, values clarification, decision-making, and SAT preparation. Students are paired with adult mentors. These mentors can answer questions about college and the workforce, as well as serving as role models.

Over the course of the summer following their junior year, students undergo an enrichment program that meets once a week for six weeks. Topics explored relate to those covered during the school year, but with a focus on post-secondary education and employment. Areas of interest might include career choices, study skills, or time management, or students might attend a mini college fair.

Monthly meetings are held throughout the senior year. In the fall, issues of college admission and financial aid are the focus. In the spring, college survival skills are discussed. Mentors and parents are strongly encouraged to become actively involved with their students and the Career Beginnings program during the last two years of high school.

Another important aspect of Career Beginnings is the casework approach that is undertaken. A staff member of the SAC must track the students in the program. The staff member must seek out bimonthly updates from these students, monitoring their grades and college admissions processes. Additional program information can be found in Appendix 4.

Other Programs

The goal of the Student Assistance Center and its ancillary programs is to involve as many students as possible in the wide range of programs offered. Self-esteem, peer acceptance, and connection with an institution are all fostered by participation in these activities.

In East Hartford, students have flocked to the seminars on the topics of nutrition and relationships. A young man ashamed to go to any school activity for fear of being ridiculed because of his weight attended a series of these programs on nutrition and now is trying out for the color guard squad.

Other program ideas include:

- ♦ A study-skills program
- ♦ Health presentations
- ♦ Relationship-oriented meetings
- ♦ Alternatives to study halls
- ♦ Presentations by career practitioners and specialists

Many times, students will come up with important, creative, much-needed programs in which they would like to participate. Paramount to remember, an SAC should reflect the varying needs and unique aspects of the school and its community.

Chapter 6

Support Services and Agencies

School-Based Health Center
Police Outreach
Probation
Department of Children and Families
The Governor's Prevention Partnership
Other Agencies and Community Resources

Developing a successful Student Assistance Program takes the cooperation of numerous outside agencies. The SAC itself serves as the nucleus while the other agencies tend to support the center, each providing technical and specialized assistance when needed. This structure allows the SAC to expand services and to integrate programs throughout the community. Some internal and external organizations critical to the functioning of the center are highlighted here. Each institution should develop its own unique manual of community support agencies that is updated regularly.

School-Based Health Center

The School-Based Health Center (SBHC) provides on-site physical and mental health care services to students within the school setting. Typically, it is staffed by one or more nurse practitioners, a social worker, and a drug and alcohol counselor. The director of the SBHC and the coordinator of the SAC work cooperatively to enhance the mental and physical health of students.

While the school still maintains a nurse's office, the SBHC receives referrals from the school nurses, as well as walk-in visitors and students who have been recommended by the SAC staff. The SBHC has the advantage of being aligned with a hospital and has admitting privileges. This allows for prompt medical care for children who would not likely seek such assistance for financial reasons or parental oversight, as well as providing quicker response time in medical emergencies.

The effectiveness of the SBHC in an emergency situation is underscored here: A 14-year-old student approached an SAC staff member complaining of abdominal pain and a fever. The staff member escorted the student to the SBHC. During the physical by the SBHC nurse, the student confided that she had had an abortion two days earlier. She was hemorrhaging and required immediate hospitalization. The youth was stabilized and transported to the hospital while the SAC contacted her guardian.

This is only one example of the many benefits of the SBHC. Countless school days are saved due to the availability of the services provided in the SBHC. A diagnosis is given and the treatment dispensed in the same visit, allowing the student to return to the classroom with minimal disruption of the academic day.

The SBHC is active in women's issues with pregnancy testing and educational and medical services for those students who are pregnant. In addition, the SBHC has played a critical role in the diagnosis and treatment of sexually transmitted diseases, and in the promotion of responsible sexual behavior. Beside the support and counseling services it offers for sexually active or curious teens, the SBHC also sponsors informational programs in areas such as eating disorders, weight management programs, and other health-related topics. Smoking cessation support groups sponsored by ERASE (East of the River Association for Substance-Abuse Elimination) are also available. The center's proactive approach to preventing medical problems through education and counseling that has made the SBHC an invaluable asset.

If your state doesn't provide funding for a School Based Health Center, you may be able to offer some of the services described here by collaborating with area hospitals, community-based health centers, or other providers.

Police Outreach

The Community Outreach Program in East Hartford assigns a particular police officer to a neighborhood. These officers become an integral part of the community, sometimes opening police "outposts" in that area. Police involvement should be handled carefully, as in minority neighborhoods or areas with high police-community tension charges of brutality or misconduct can make citizens wary of police. The goal is to have the residents see the officers as a resource, not as intruders. In turn, the officers become familiar with the type of crime activity that takes place in the area with the focus on prevention, rather than prosecution.

In addition to "walking the beat" in the neighborhood, the

officers regularly visit the local schools. Working cooperatively with school officials, they have become part of a team to undermine local violence and criminal activity. Below, East Hartford Community Outreach Officer Peter Slocum describes the valuable, symbiotic relationship forged between the police and the high school community:

> There is an on-going and excellent partnership between the SAC and the Police Department Community Outreach Division. As a resource officer in the high school, I have constant contact with students who are referred to me by the SAC. In turn students have been referred by me to SAC to take advantage of the many counseling services provided there.
>
> This practice of cross referrals helps to identify those students in need of friendly advice and/or help. In this day of heightened awareness in schools, it is crucial that all threats and disturbing behavior be thoroughly investigated. Case in point: a staff member became concerned regarding the cavalier comments about violence that a student made in class. Furthermore, the student boasted about his penchant for carrying weapons. The SAC notified security and myself. Follow-up investigation revealed that the student had a razor-blade knife in his school locker. The student was arrested and a potentially deadly weapon was removed from the school.
>
> In another case, several students reported to the SAC that a non-student in an alternative incarceration program threatened to do a drive-by shooting on this group. The alarming details about this case were that the potential shooter targeted a specific date during a long holiday weekend when he would be on furlough, and his anger stemmed from the breakup with a female he was obsessed with. Further investigation was done and statements were taken from students who were present when the threats were made. The offender's probation officer was notified. He was referred to juvenile court and all weekend furloughs were cancelled. This intervention would not have been possible if the group of students had not come forward to the SAC.

This type of relationship doesn't happen overnight, but with hard work, patience, and understanding cooperation from the local authorities, police can be useful allies in keeping our schools safe.

This outreach division of the police department is both partner and necessary adjunct to the public school system in the new millennium; and it is particularly welcome in urban schools like East Hartford, as these comments by students to East Hartford Principal Steven Edwards attest:

Dr. Edwards: Tom, what do you think—are there advantages or disadvantages of outreach officers in school?

Tom: It could be both an advantage or disadvantage. Some people don't like cops, but I think it is a plus because Officer Slocum is just a perfect guy to talk to, he gets along with kids, and I just hear all good comments about him. I think it also makes kids feel a little safe here. Like in [other towns] I don't think they have any cops in their school. I have friends there and they say, "Well, you have a cop in your school?" and I say, "Yes, it makes some of us feel a little safer." It's not to say that school shoots are not going to happen or anything. I know there have been some weapons brought into this school, but it makes you feel a little safer.

Dr. Edwards: Darrell, what are your thoughts on outreach officers in the schools?

Darrell: It is good to know that you can feel safe in school, you know, to see him. You know what happened in Columbine or whatever, and that's a real tragedy, so its more like a comfort. Even though there is a lot of conflict going on and somebody could snap at any moment, so it's just good to see a security officer.

Dr. Edwards: Do you feel that the police officer works well with students?

Darrell: Sure, he gets to know a lot of students, therefore it prevents a lot of fights from happening.

Dr. Edwards: Suliaman, what do you think about outreach officers in the school?

Suliaman: Protection.

Dr. Edwards: You've talked to Officer Slocum before. What have been your experiences?

Suliaman: He has let me know what it is like being a police officer, and what he does here. Basically what his action is in school, because people know Slocum well, so they aren't gonna bring nothing in school. They know that people will tell on them, so it shows them not to mess around with it.

The SAC staff works closely with the police, who are already aware of the pressures facing the children, both at school and on the streets. This sharing of information between the SAC staff and police helps prevent a multitude of potential problems.

In one case, an officer working his neighborhood came upon information that two rival gangs were planning a showdown at an upcoming Friday evening football game. The officer informed his supervisor who, in turn, contacted the school. In cooperation with the police, the school mobilized its resources in the SAC, developing an action plan to defuse, through dialogue, a potentially volatile situation.

The officers work cooperatively with SAC staff members in conflict-management, violence prevention groups, and classroom discussions. They are an integral part of the day-to-day operation of the SAC and provide valuable support services to staff and students.

Probation

An area of growing concern is addressing the needs of students on court probation as a result of prior convictions. Typically, the student on probation would meet with the probation officer at an off-campus location. But the SAC, in cooperation with local probation officials, established a program where the probation officer comes to the school to meet with the student in the SAC offices. Bimonthly appointments are arranged, and the probation officer, student, and SAC staff member meet together.

The advantages to this setup are significant. The SAC staffer has a complete biographical sketch of the child and can share timely information at the meeting regarding academic progress, behavior, attendance, and other pertinent information. In addition, criteria regarding school performance can become part of the youth's conditions of probation.

The student now sees that the school and court systems are working hand-in-hand, thereby providing more efficient, comprehensive monitoring and help during difficult times.

Department of Children and Families

The Department of Children and Families (DCF), the state of Connecticut's child protection agency, is another organization that has fallen under the umbrella of the SAC for children who are under foster care or are receiving other services from DCF.

The arrangement with the DCF and the SAC is similar to that of the Police Outreach Program. When the need arises, a Department of Children and Families caseworker will meet with the student and an SAC staff member. This allows for the school's perspective to be presented at the meeting, while at the same time, representing the child's and the DCF's positions.

The Governor's Prevention Partnership

Another program in Connecticut that promotes healthy minds and bodies is The Governor's Prevention Partnership, founded for the prevention of substance abuse among the present and future workforce in the state of Connecticut. This program evolved from the efforts of a dedicated partnership between private industry and the state government.

The SAC staff has made use of the many resources available through The Governor's Prevention Partnership. Although this is a Connecticut-based program, it is likely that other states have a counterpart with a comparable mission that can be utilized.

Other Agencies and Community Resources

Other community agencies working closely with the SAC in East Hartford include:

- Rotary
- Partners in Business
- Parent Teacher Organization
- Youth Services
- Child Plan
- YMCA
- State Department of Social Services
- ERASE
- Town of East Hartford
- Board of Education
- University of Connecticut, School of Education
- University of Connecticut, School of Social Work
- University of Connecticut, Cultural Center
- Tunxis Community College
- East Hartford Police Department, Community Outreach Program

Most cities and towns have local counterparts to these East Hartford groups. The programs and resources used by your SAC will depend on the needs of your students and the resources in your community. Some possible places to look for support:

- Business community
- Civic and community groups
- Educators
- General public
- Parents
- Public officials
- Religious community
- Media and agencies

Chapter 7

Winning Your Public

Marketing to Educators
Getting the Word Out
Sharing Your Success

The purpose of the Student Assistance Center is to help students reach their learning potential safely and peacefully. The core of the SAC's proactive approach is based on two primary objectives for effective discipline as identified by educators Grassnichle and Sesko (1985, 48):

1. Assist the student in understanding him or herself, goals, feelings, aspirations, and the relationship of school and learning to those factors.

2. Identify alternative behaviors that are acceptable to teachers, administrators, and peers. It is important that these behaviors are acceptable to the youth's parents or guardians as well.

Marketing to Educators

In laying the groundwork for an SAC, first gain the support of the principals and administrators at a proposed site. A well-run SAC will offer a variety of services that traditionally fall under the auspices of several different departments; the SAC is run most efficiently with support from the top to help to limit or circumvent territorial struggles that might otherwise occur in the face of a new program.

The next step is to lobby department heads, the guidance department, and teachers. Soliciting the support, understanding, and input of the faculty is vitally important. The Student Assistance Center is an adjunct to existing programs, not a replacement for any department. The faculty should be given an opportunity to identify critical school issues to be addressed. They are also needed to refer students and staff to the SAC and the Student Assistance Team. Feeling they had a voice in the SAC's creation will mean teachers and staff feel involved in its success.

Winning SAC support from faculty and staff requires assurance that formal and informal educational protocol is followed. Rules should be posted in the SAC reminding students that visits there do not excuse them from their classroom obligations, including the responsibility to explain their absence to their classroom teacher, submit work that is due, and ascertain all class notes, assignments, and homework due dates. Such reinforcement of school policy prevents classroom teachers from feeling their authority is being usurped or the students are working the system.

For those concerned about lost classroom time for students who go to the SAC, what must be weighed is whether that student, in the throes of anger or psychic pain, would even be able to focus at all on academics at that point. Of greater concern is the very real potential for that student to become disruptive or confrontational, if forced to remain in class. Then it is not the lost class time for just one student; it is the valuable learning time lost for each and every student in that room, as the classroom teacher attempts to deal with the disruption. Sometimes, returning the class's attention to the lesson becomes impossible and frustrating for faculty and students alike.

While certain departments will be very receptive, others, such as the guidance and social work areas, may need more convincing. It is important they are included in this process. Because of sheer student numbers, rather than any inherent inadequacies, these two support groups are unable to meet the burgeoning complex demands of our youth and those of the educational community by themselves. A recent news article on school truancy identifies the need for expanded support services. A boy who missed twenty-two days of school lamented:

> The school doesn't care. Some teachers do, and some counselors do, but they have too much to deal with. If one student doesn't want to go to class, it's like the heck with it. (Green 1997, B1)

This is where the Student Assistance Center fits in.

Getting the Word Out

To accomplish the SAC's goals, students, staff, teachers, and parents and guardians must first be aware of the center's existence, its programming, and its many uses. Before the start of school, students and their parents need to be educated about the SAC and the positive contribution that it can make to their lives.

An orientation program should be presented for students at the end of their eighth-grade year or during the summer before they enter high school to introduce the programs that make up the SAC, including program literature for parents to take home.

Reinforce this message when the school year begins. Freshman orientation should be conducted by the SAC during study halls, where groups of about ten students are called to the center and reintroduced to the mission of the program. Stress the availability and confidentiality of services as well as the wide scope of the SAC programs available to these new students. In addition, Student Interest Questionnaires (Appendix 15) may be distributed at this time to determine what students like to do outside of school. The purpose of the Student Interest Questionnaire is to develop new activities and to tailor existing after-school programs, to which students may be directed.

Parents are a particularly valuable asset for a fully functioning referral system. An orientation for parents is recommended and can be conducted at a back-to-school night program. Bringing parents into the school and providing them with information about the program establishes a referral system—in essence, a conduit through which parents can raise and address their concerns. Once parents know their input is valued and welcomed, they will be more forthcoming with concerns.

Sharing Your Success

Once a successful program has been built, the experiences associated with the construction and maintenance of that format should be shared with other schools seeking to create similar programs. By serving as consultants to other schools, SAC directors also serve their own programs' purposes. They will, no doubt, come into contact with other schools attempting to implement new ideas that may be added to their own center.

While this type of inter-agency involvement ensures some amount of local recognition, a wider field of influence can be gained through media attention. The first step is to start an SAC newsletter or to participate with an existing school publication. Not only does this maintain communication within the school community, it also provides a written account of SAC events that can be sent as briefings to local newspapers.

Innovative student assistance programs that reduce violence, increase student productivity, and build self-esteem should be chronicled in the press. Reporters at local newspapers and television stations are always looking for stories; a successful SAC that is addressing real issues can provide them, and some reporters will become interested and follow the story over time. Keep the press informed of your events and accomplishments with news releases that contain concrete information and results. Recognize reporters who are interested and who understand the issues and keep them in the loop.

Further, involvement and membership in specific organizations such as the National Association for Secondary School Principals (NASSP), National Association for Mediators in Education (NAME), and Educators for Social Responsibility (ESR) will help ensure that programs are centered on timely educational issues as well as on trend-setting ideas and resource information.

Successful initiatives of one school may help to actualize change in another school simply by serving as a model, demonstrating the level of excellence that this educational system is capable of attaining.

Chapter 8

Funding

Given the wide range of services that a well-run Student Assistant Center will provide, the cost of starting and running a program is relatively low. Nevertheless, proper funding is necessary.

Expenses will include the initial peer mediation training session, capital outlay such as furniture, and annual expenses like the director's salary and office supplies. It is essential that stable funding is secured to sustain the program once it has been established.

The first place to look for funding is within the school community. Present to your local school board the need for a program, outlining potential benefits and projected outcomes. This is the body with the greatest stake in your school's success. Be sure to stress the comprehensive impact a successful SAC can have on violence prevention and student achievement, presenting a holistic and proven approach to the problem.

In addition, local, state, and national organizations, outside the community and educational systems, should also be considered for additional funding. Local universities and businesses are good places to start. Service programs, whose goals are to aid and improve the local community, are a good source of support.

Universities may provide the skilled staffing that is needed but that the school cannot afford. Mutually beneficial relationships between public schools and colleges should be encouraged and cultivated. College interns volunteer time in exchange for opportunities to practice and foster their skills in a school setting.

Local businesses may provide funding or goods, such as furniture and office materials. An SAC can benefit greatly from the help and attention of a corporate sponsor willing to supply manpower, money, or advice, and mentors, advisors, or just good listeners; this is a way a company can demonstrate its commitment to keeping our communities safe and our schools free of violence. Be sure to tell them when making your pitch that you will publicize their contributions in newsletters, on a plaque in your building, or any other way that will work for you. Businesses love to have their contributions recognized and their generosity with community projects publically acknowledged.

Grants

When searching for funding on the state or national level, first get an idea of available state and federal grants; these will help to evaluate what is available and how to qualify. Don't be afraid to go on the Internet and spend some time searching. Many schools and towns also have a grant writing position; yours may already have the detailed demographic information required for many grant applications, or be willing to write or assist in grantwriting proposals. In Connecticut, state agencies such as the Department of Social Services or the State Department of Education are good sources of funding. Your state will have others.

Also, there are many corporations and foundations interested in social change and helping the community. Find out their qualifications and get to know them. Invite them to tour your program, even if they have just turned down your application. Show them what you are accomplishing, and they may well become interested later.

East Hartford High School's SAC Funding

Director's salary is outside the teacher ratio	Varies
Social worker provided by school system	Varies
Furniture is donated	$0
Part-time drug counselor	$15,000
funded by a grant from Drug-Free Schools	
Career Beginnings, peer mediation training,	$13,000
supervision, and transportation	
funded by a grant from the Connecticut	
State Department of Social Services	
Town and Board of Education funding (varies yearly)	$4,900
Miscellaneous donations	$1,000
Total funding without staff salaries	$33,900

Record Keeping

Most grant applications will ask for statistics and demographics that reflect the need for your program. It is also vital to compile and maintain statistics that track the effects of your SAC. Facts and figures that demonstrate the effect of an intervention program need to be collected. Information of particular relevance to Student Assistance Center programs is the rate of suspensions and expulsions before and after the implementation of the SAC. Others to consider, based on your community and your goals, are dropout rates, teenage pregnancy, percentage of athletes maintaining good grades, and student involvement in the community.

Statistical analysis should not be underestimated. It can make a powerful statement about the effectiveness of your program, and funders will listen. Regular surveys of participants can point out areas for improvement as well as documenting your success. (See sample Substance Abuse Survey, Appendix 14.)

Accurate record-keeping is essential. Most private and public agencies, including school boards and state departments of education, require specific documentation of need and stringent statistical analysis of program successes. Comparative statistical analysis—that is, a year-to-year comparison of relevant factors—is essential for the initial and continuous funding of adjunct programs.

Data about a program should be gathered conscientiously and responsibly with an eye toward statistical reliability and validity. The fiscal success of the SAC, as well as for the entire students-at-risk program, may depend on this.

Chapter 9

The SAC's Success

Since the Student Assistance Center's implementation in East Hartford in 1993, student involvement in the program has climbed to over 4,000, with about 600 new students served yearly. This active, positive participation of students attests to both the need for and acceptance of the SAC in the educational community. In the SAC's first year, detentions and suspensions at East Hartford High plummeted from 2,570 to 1,438.

This dramatic 44-percent decrease in educationally disruptive acts has helped establish a school climate that is both safe and conducive to learning. This significant decrease continues to be maintained despite the sharp rise in East Hartford High School's population from 1,400 to over 2,200 in just eight years; that is a 75-percent rise in the student body, coming from increasingly socio-economically deprived households.

Through the implementation of the SAC, class-cutting and truancy had dropped 70 percent by 1995. Equally significant, the instances of physical violence have maintained a 35-percent reduction since the SAC's inception.

These impressive statistics are in part due to the connections students feel with the center and the members of the SAC staff. Making connections is what the SAC is all about. Establishing and sustaining one-to-one relationships is so necessary in developing healthy socialization skills. The empowerment of their peers as student mediators appears to be a key factor in student acceptance of the SAC programs. Here is "grassroots" democracy in action, a tribute to our tradition of equality and mutual respect.

Students who have reaped the benefit of the SAC report experiencing a great sense of belonging with the high school, improved peer acceptance, and enhanced self-esteem. "It's nice to have someone you can trust," one student shared. "I've been in counseling since, like, second grade, and I just started to open up in this group a few years ago."

Others cite improvement in their anger management skills, saying they are less likely now to let anger control their actions. The SAC helps individuals resolve conflicts through a productive process that focuses on what can be done in the future, rather than what has happened in the past. This itself leads to effective solutions that help to curb violence.

Reflecting on the help the SAC has been to police and their interaction with troubled youth, an officer observed, "If they didn't come here, we'd be getting involved in the streets or in the halls."

Hindsight

The potential for violence is a painful reality for teenagers who have made poor choices. And it is no longer restricted to boys, as the Williamsport, Pennsylvania, shooting by a 14-year-old girl illustrates (Morris, 28). To capture the sad complexities of some of our students emotionally charged world, here is an essay by a girl whose unfortunate gang affiliation with the Latin Queens turned her senior year upside-down.

Reliving Last Year

Many things have happened last year. There are a lot of memories that I still hold with me. But there is one that will always be with me and I'll never forget.

I came from Hartford where I was born and raised. I studied in [an urban school] my four years of high school. Unfortunately my senior year I decided to do a big mistake. I joined the Latin Queens. A gang. I joined the gang for three months, when I realized it wasn't for me. Going around hurting people, selling drugs, and many other things wasn't something I wanted to continue. So I stopped going to my meetings and hanging out with them. The day came when some guys and girls came to my house looking for me. They set me up and managed to convince me we were going to hang out. Instead it turned out to be to an abandoned building where four girls beat me up. I was hurt. I had bruises, black eyes, scratches, and aches and pains. I was in bed for two weeks and couldn't go back to school to take my final exams. Yes, I was eligible to go to summer school, but the worst wasn't over.

Since I didn't end up in the hospital, hospitalized, they decided the damage to me wasn't enough. Rumors were they wanted me in critical condition. They were constantly going to my house looking for me—morning, noon, and night. I was unable to go outside or be seen. After debating with my family on what to do with me, we decided to send me back to Puerto Rico.

It still wasn't over. They kept looking for me because they didn't know where I was. They finally found out and stopped looking for me. I was undecided on whether to come back to the states or stay in Puerto Rico because my safety was first. Deciding to come back to the states everyone found out. So once again the girls were looking for me. So my family decided to go to East Hartford to live. Now I'm in East Hartford High with a different name....I work with an undercover cop in school, and I say I come from Puerto Rico. It's frustrating being unable to reveal your past. Thinking about how long ago this was and happened it is still not over. Regrets, regrets only, that's all I have.

Chapter 10

Conclusion

Conflict does not always have to end in violence, but violence always begins with conflict. Schools must be proactive in their approach to dealing with both.

A Student Assistance Center is designed to address conflict before it becomes violent. It is our job as parents and educators to recognize the warning signs and face them head on. The children of Columbine and Santana grew up too soon. Our society cannot endure another massacre.

But there is hope. At East Hartford High School, we have found it in a "sea-change" in students' abilities to participate in their own mediation of conflict. These new programs really work!

Against a backdrop of raging hormones and hardcore song lyrics, our youth are developing faster than ever before. Add to the mix an increase in absentee parenting, the growing number of children raised in dysfunctional homes or involved in toxic relationships, and public schools face an unprecedented challenge.

America's love affair with the handgun, violent video games that mete out explosions as punishment and revenge as their goal, explicit violence in movies, games, advertising, and music. All these create an atmosphere in which often the first reaction to conflict that comes to mind is violence. And it isn't just youth culture that perpetuates the violence. While movies and games—produced by adults—portray violence in fantasy settings, adults, role models for children, continue to act it out in real life, and our children follow the example. Parents murder each other at little-league games; respected members of communities beat their spouses and children; state governments respond by executing prisoners; and the U.S. and other nations' governments bomb each others' hospitals and schools.

From state and national policy to the most private social issues, violence is increasingly used as the solution to problems. None of the old rules seem to apply. We are facing the demons of our increasingly violent, desensitized, and materialistic society, which has brought with it growing disillusionment and fear. Our students are almost numb to the violence that engulfs us, and unless it is one of our children who perpetrates a horrible act of violence, we adults are often as desensitized as are our youth.

The warning of AIDS activist and victim Elizabeth Glaser is sadly prophetic: "America has lost her path. She's at risk of losing her soul. Wake up, America!"

Schools are supposed to be safe. To ensure that they are, educators must return to the basics of discipline, respect, and focused academics—teaching and learning. Authoritarian discipline, however, imposed from above does not work well; and therein lies the value of the SAC: *We empower the students themselves with peacekeeping skills and decision-making power.*

That is our "secret" weapon—and that is the key ingredient of East Hartford High School's Student Assistance Center, outlined here, that will make these steps successful in other communities. We must continue to empower youth. We must be alert to the signs and the potential for violence. We must neither ignore nor trivialize the outcasts among us and the pain of exclusion; we must also recognize that violence is often the outgrowth of long-standing alienation. We must not allow cruelty, teasing, or bullying under any circumstances. The cost is too high—for the victim and for the entire community.

Parents need to make time to get to know their children, and allow their children to get to know them. Parents, students and teachers must report signs of trouble without fear of retribution or humiliation. Students need a place to defuse. Teachers need to teach tolerance and compassion—in deed, as well as in word. They also need a place to send students who appear to be in need, where feelings of alienation or hopelessness can be confronted, where disputes can be aired and rumors put to rest, where friends can refer friends who are troubled, teased, or otherwise tormented. We must remind our students—and ourselves—that we truly are our brothers' keepers.

If schools have indeed become surrogate parents, it is our duty as parents to keep our children safe. It is our mission as educators to make them safe both physically and emotionally. A Student Assistance Center provides a safe haven, and it works.

Appendix **1**

Student Assistance Center Timeline

Determine a need for the program. Be sure to include all facets of the school and community. Include the following in your timeline: administrative support, logistics, and financial backing.

I. Determine a need for the program.
    A. Obtain administrative support.
    B. Appoint a director or administrator.
    C. Form a steering committee:
        1. Administration
        2. Staff
        3. Community
        4. Students
    D. The steering subcommittee should visit other established programs:
        1. Compare scope and needs.
        2. Gather information.
        3. Visit a total of three programs.
        4. Summarize observations and report back to the steering committee.
    E. Distribute needs survey to determine the specific needs of the individual institution. Categories should include the following:
        1. Drug and alcohol
        2. Careers
        3. Conflict resolution
        4. Mediation
        5. Student assistance
    F. Secure continuous financial backing.
    G. Locate positive logistical setting.
    H. Obtain staff approval through marketing.
    I. Orient students to the program's components. This is a major key to success.
    J. Use myriad community resources.
    K. Formulate staffing procedures.
    L. Develop a mission statement.
II. The scope and focus of the program should suit the institution it serves.
    A. The steering committee should assist on categories C through L on the time line.
    B. Follow through on I and determine a need for the program.
    C. Allow three to five years to establish and develop a mature system.
    D. Implementation of any component will take from three to six months to reach fruition.

Appendix 2

Student Assistance Center
Needs-Assessment Survey *

This is an important piece in the orientation of all freshmen. Students will be more open in this confidential document. Keep this on file!

Please check off and/or write in your answer to the following:

Male ☐   Female ☐   Age _____

Do you exhibit or have concerns in any of the following areas?

	Always True	Usually True	Usually False	Always False
1. I have good relationships with my teachers.	☐	☐	☐	☐
2. I am a hard and steady worker at school.	☐	☐	☐	☐
3. I'm popular with other kids my age.	☐	☐	☐	☐
4. I'm good at schoolwork.	☐	☐	☐	☐
5. My home life is pretty pleasant.	☐	☐	☐	☐
6. Kids pick on me a lot.	☐	☐	☐	☐
7. I am good about doing my homework on time.	☐	☐	☐	☐
8. It's easy for me to make friends.	☐	☐	☐	☐
9. I often feel ashamed of myself.	☐	☐	☐	☐
10. I'm proud of my schoolwork.	☐	☐	☐	☐
11. My parents don't listen to me.	☐	☐	☐	☐
12. My friends don't have much confidence in me.	☐	☐	☐	☐
13. I can go to my parents with my problems.	☐	☐	☐	☐
14. I don't have trouble talking to other people.	☐	☐	☐	☐
15. I like going to school.	☐	☐	☐	☐
16. I give the teachers a lot of trouble at school.	☐	☐	☐	☐
17. I never feel like I'm part of the group.	☐	☐	☐	☐
18. My parents are disappointed in my school grades.	☐	☐	☐	☐
19. Most days I don't feel like doing anything.	☐	☐	☐	☐
20. I have difficulty paying attention.	☐	☐	☐	☐
21. I get into trouble for things that aren't my fault.	☐	☐	☐	☐
22. I get along with my peers.	☐	☐	☐	☐

* Note: Some questions were adapted from the Self-Esteem Index, Copyright 1990, PRO-ED, Inc.

Needs Assessment Survey (continued)

	Always True	Usually True	Usually False	Always False
23. I spend time alone, separate from others.	☐	☐	☐	☐
24. I fail at most things I try.	☐	☐	☐	☐
25. I include other people in my plans.	☐	☐	☐	☐
26. I follow the rules of the school.	☐	☐	☐	☐
27. I exaggerate my troubles in order to get attention.	☐	☐	☐	☐
28. My moods change frequently.	☐	☐	☐	☐
29. I use obscene language to describe how I am feeling.	☐	☐	☐	☐
30. Other kids think I am a crybaby.	☐	☐	☐	☐
31. My behavior at school is okay.	☐	☐	☐	☐
32. Nobody pays much attention to me at home.	☐	☐	☐	☐
33. I think I'm pretty easy to like.	☐	☐	☐	☐
34. I do as little work at school as I can get by with.	☐	☐	☐	☐
35. I like being with other kids.	☐	☐	☐	☐
36. I'm not doing as well in school as I'd like to.	☐	☐	☐	☐
37. My family will help me if I get into trouble.	☐	☐	☐	☐
38. It's hard to work in classrooms that have a lot of rules.	☐	☐	☐	☐
39. Friends let me take the blame for things they have done.	☐	☐	☐	☐
40. When angry, I get into fights.	☐	☐	☐	☐
41. I argue a lot with my peers.	☐	☐	☐	☐
42. My teachers like me.	☐	☐	☐	☐
43. Sometimes I play sick to get out of school.	☐	☐	☐	☐
44. I learn a lot from other people.	☐	☐	☐	☐
45. People in my family have quick tempers.	☐	☐	☐	☐
46. It's fun to learn new things.	☐	☐	☐	☐
47. I brag about my drug use.	☐	☐	☐	☐
48. Things at home upset me.	☐	☐	☐	☐
49. I don't have trouble making up my mind about things.	☐	☐	☐	☐
50. I have friends I can confide in.	☐	☐	☐	☐

Appendix 3

Student Assistance Center
Set-Up—Architectural Design / Logistics

The Student Assistance Center is best located in an accessible area with the capability of private conference areas.

	Hallway	
Drug and Alcohol Group		Peer Mediation Groups
	Lobby	
Administration		Social Work

LOGISTICAL SPECIFICATIONS

1. User-Friendly, Conducive, Appealing
2. At Least Two Rooms for Cooling-Down Process
3. Comfortable Furniture, Couch, Pictures, Rugs
4. Literature Table in Lobby
5. Specific Areas Designated with Signs

Appendix 4

Help Shape the Future

Be a mentor to a Hartford high school student
through Career Beginnings

In conjunction with the Guidance program, this enables high-maintenance students to achieve optimum success.

Hartford Career Beginnings pairs each participating student with a volunteer adult mentor. Mentors help to guide students through the college admissions process by offering the benefit of their experiences. Mentors also help students to understand what level of education is necessary in order to achieve career goals. Mentors are trained in the role by a full-time mentor coordinator who provides orientation and ongoing counseling and support. Mentors provide a critical connection to the world of higher education and employment and help Hartford teenagers realize that they are part of a community of citizens who care.

A good mentor is someone who:

- wishes to offer a helping hand to a Hartford teenager
- recognizes the value of a mentor relationship
- wishes to share expertise
- has had some college education
- is self confident and resourceful
- can spend a minimum of five hours per month with a student
- can make a commitment for one year

Mentors assists students with:

- the college selection and application process
- setting educational and career goals
- academic counseling and encouragement
- information about college life
- career options and planning

For more information call Lucy Carmona, Career Beginnings Mentor Coordinator, at 233-3915, located on the campus of Saint Joseph College, 1678 Asylum Avenue, West Hartford, CT 06117. Career Beginnings is an initiative of the Hartford Consortium for Higher Education.

Appendix *5*

Mediation Agreement Form *

This form is essential in the culmination of any successful mediation. Should be kept on file for any future use.

Date: _____   Case #: _____

_____   _____
Disputant   Disputant

_____   _____
Disputant   Disputant

_____   _____
Student Mediator   Student Mediator

_____   _____
Student Mediator   Staff Mediator

****
AGREEMENT: _____

_____

_____

_____

_____

_____

All parties to this agreement, please sign on appropriate line:

_____   _____
Disputant   Disputant

_____   _____
Disputant   Disputant

_____   _____
Student Mediator   Student Mediator

_____   _____
Student Mediator   Staff Mediator
****
FOLLOW-UP

Date: _____   Person Doing Follow-up: _____

Results: _____

_____

Comments: _____

_____

* Form used by CMI, Inc.

Appendix 6

Peer Mediation Application

(Questionnaire for Potential Peer Mediation)

To ensure proper balance between the mediators and the school population.
Also a check for the sincerity of the applicant.

1. Name: _____

2. Age: _____ 3. Grade: _____ 4. Race: _____

5. Languages spoken: _____

6. Times available: _____

SITUATIONAL QUESTIONS
How would you handle the following situations?

7. Fight: Two students are referred to Peer Mediation due to punching each
other in a dispute over an ex-girlfriend.

8. Anorexia: A female student comes to speak with you about her friend who is
anorexic. She is very worried about her friend because she denies being anorexic
and won't seek help.

9. Pregnancy: A female comes to you and tells you that she thinks she's pregnant. She is scared to death and doesn't know what to do.

10. Stealing: Two males are referred to Peer Mediation by a teacher because one
is accusing the other of stealing his coat; the accused denies it.

11. Threats: Two students threaten each other and are suspected of planning to
fight after school gets out. A teacher overhears them and sends them to Peer
Mediation.

12. What qualities can you bring to this program?

13. Are you willing to commit yourself to the time involved in becoming a Peer
Mediator—20 hours of training (possibly on weekends), attending meetings,
and taking time out during the school day to peer mediate?
          Yes ☐   No ☐   Need to think about further ☐

Appendix *7*

Overview of
Student Assistance Team Procedures

Vital for recordkeeping and accessibility. Must be reviewed by every person involved on the Student Assistance Team.

> ➤ Referral Cards (green) located in the teacher's mailroom and Student Assistance Center (SAC).

> ➤ After Referral Cards are completed, they are to be put into a locked box in the teachers' mail room (keys located in SAC office). Cards will be picked up daily and distributed in individual SAT members' mailboxes.

> ➤ Student Intake Cards (blue) will be distributed in individual SAT members' mailboxes.

> ➤ When an SAT member receives an Intake Card, he/she will proceed to the SAC office where he/she will find the corresponding Referral Card in a labeled manila file folder. Referral Cards and folders are found in a locked two-drawer file cabinet. (Keys in middle drawer of desk).

> ➤ SAT member will then gather background information from social worker, nurse, guidance, assistant principal, etc.

> ➤ At the SAT member's convenience, he/she will set up a meeting with the referred student.

> ➤ After meeting with the referred student, the Intake Card will be filled out and returned to the locked file cabinet in the SAC office.

> ➤ At this point, the SAT member, to the best of his/her knowledge, will try to understand the student's problem, try to formulate some type of solution, and then try to expedite a program for that youth.

> ➤ A teacher reply card (yellow) must then be completed and returned to the staff member who referred the student to the Student Assistance Team.

> ➤ A six-week update by staff must be completed (check back with student and teacher).

> ➤ While progressing through the SAT cycle, please place colored dots on the student's folder to indicate which steps have been completed.

Appendix **8**

SAC Referral Form *

First step in the Student Assistance Team procedure (green card). These cards should be placed in areas throughout the building that are convenient to all staff and students.

Student's Name: _____

Date: _____ House: _____ Grade: _____

Name of person making referral: _____

(Your name will not be shared outside the Student Assistance Team without your permission).

Reason for referral/Behaviors of concern: _____

_____

_____

_____

_____

_____

_____

_____

_____

_____

* Form used by The Governor's Prevention Partnership.

Appendix 9

Behaviors of Concern *

This is included (on back of green card) with an indication of the problem.

☐ Decline in quality of work
☐ Erratic behavior day to day
☐ Inattentiveness
☐ Decline in grade earned
☐ Lack of motivation
☐ Mood swings
☐ Withdrawal, a loner; separates from others
☐ Extreme negativeness
☐ Incomplete work
☐ Defiance of authority
☐ Defiance, breaking the rules
☐ Defensiveness
☐ Work not handed in
☐ Talks freely about alcohol/drug use; bragging
☐ Hyperactivity; nervousness
☐ Failing in this subject _____
☐ Other students express concern about possible problem
☐ Verbally abusive
☐ Physically abusive
☐ Frequently needs discipline
☐ Potentially violent

Other concerns or comments: _____

_____

_____

_____

_____

Six-Week Update: _____

_____

_____

_____

* Adapted from The Governor's Prevention Partnership.

Appendix 1 0

Student Assistance Center
Intake Form *

This Second Step (Blue Card) to be used by SAT staffer. Information to be entered in client's folder and placed in a secure area.

Student's Name: _____

Name of Intake: _____

Date Received: _____

Action Taken: _____

_____

_____

_____

_____

_____

_____

_____

_____

* From The Governor's Prevention Partnership.

Appendix **11**

Student Assistance Center
Reply Form *

Third and final step (yellow card) to be returned to the individual who referred the student to the SAC. A critical step to ensure the lines of communication are open.

Dear _____

Thank you for referring _____ to the SAC.

We would like to inform you that we have met this student and the following actions have been taken:

_____

_____

_____

_____

_____

If you have further questions, please contact the SAT at extension _____ or_____, or stop by to see us. We are located at the north end of the Media Center.

Sincerely,

SAT

* From The Governor's Prevention Partnership.

Appendix 12

East Hartford High School
Confidential Alert List

This list helps ensure smooth transition from 8th grade to 9th grade. A proactive approach that assists in the formation of a positive connection.

Date: _____

Student ID#:	Student Name:	Areas of Concern:

Appendix 13

Drug and Alcohol Insight Group

The group enables students who might be having some difficulty with substance abuse to share ideas with other students.

There is a mandatory Drug and Alcohol Insight Group for those students who violate the alcohol and drug policy. This is an overview of the topics of the six-week group that addresses the following:

1. Facts on alcohol and drugs

2. Effects of alcohol and drugs on the family

3. Effects of alcohol and drugs on society

4. The addiction process

5. Oral presentations by students

6. Processing of presentations/closure for those completing the group

In addition to individual and group counseling, we offer groups specifically for children of alcoholics. An Alcoholics Anonymous meeting is also available at East Hartford High School during the school day. This is a bona fide AA meeting led by young AA presenters.

Appendix 14

Substance Abuse Survey

Important in the attainment of data used to evaluate the effect of your program.

Name (optional): _____

Grade: _____   Male ☐   Female ☐

Please write a brief response to the following questions.

1. Why do you think we need drug and alcohol counseling in this school?

2. How do you feel drug and alcohol counseling has helped you?

3. Would you recommend drug and alcohol counseling to a friend? <u>Why?</u>

4. What do you most want others to know about drug and alcohol counseling?

5. What do you <u>most like</u> about drug and alcohol counseling?

6. What do you <u>most dislike</u> about drug and alcohol counseling?

7. What affect has drug and alcohol counseling had on your life in school? Out of school?

Appendix 15

Student Interest Questionnaire

Key ingredient in the transformation and acceptance by an institution. All 9th graders are interviewed and given this questionnaire.

The Student Assistance Team is here to help YOU!

Name: _____ Birthday: _____

Favorite subject: _____

Least favorite subject: _____

INTERESTS (Please indicate if you are active in any of these):

Clubs? _____

Sports? _____

Activities? _____

Other interests? (people, places, things)

_____

_____

_____

Would you like to know more about a club or sport?

_____

_____

_____

Do you need tutoring? _____

Do you have concerns about any of your friends?

_____

_____

_____

Student Interest Questionnaire (continued)

How you felt the first day of school:

_____

_____

How you feel about school now:

_____

_____

When you think of coming to school, you:

_____

_____

You feel your teachers are:

_____

_____

If you could change anything about EHHS, what would it be?

_____

_____

_____

Do you know anyone who might need SAC assistance?

_____

_____

Please feel free to give us additional comments, concerns or advice.

_____

_____

_____

_____

_____

_____

_____

Selected Bibliography

"A Place for Every Youth in America's Schools," *School Safety Update*. National School Safety Center News Service (Nov. 1995): 1-3.

Applebombe, Peter. "Two Words Behind the Massacre," *New York Times*, Sunday, 2 May 1999, Sec. 1.

Barrows, Deborah. "Hartford Police Welcome Critical Report." *The Hartford Courant*, 12 Dec. 1999, Sec. C, 1 4(N).

Botstein, Leo. Interview on "How Schools Have Failed" on The Oprah Winfrey Show (NBC), 1 Feb. 2000.

Belcher, D. *Student Assistance Programs: The Emerging Role of Schools*. Detroit: Paper presented at Annual Meeting of the Association of Teacher Educators, 1995. (ERIC Document Reproduction Service No. ED 380 456).

Bloomfield, W. *Career Beginnings: Helping Disadvantaged Youth Achieve Their Potential*. Bloomington, Indiana: Phi Delta Kappa Educational Foundation, 1989. (ERIC Document Reproduction Service No. ED 316 618).

Boudreau, April. *I Remember the Nights*. Unpublished manuscript. 1995.

Brady, J. "Psychological Stress on Teachers Goes Way Beyond Normal Job Stress. Reprinted in *The Hartford Courant*, Sec. B4 (4N), as quoted from Shari Roan in the *Los Angeles Times*, Sec. E1.

Casale, J. *Student Assistance Program and High-Risk Youth*. Washington, DC: U.S. Department of Education, 1992. (ERIC Document Reproduction Service No. ED 364 036), 9.

Caudle, M. "Why Can't Johnny Be Safe? Eliminating School Violence." *The High School Magazine* (Sept. 1994): 10-13.

Cooley, V. "Tips for Implementing a Student Assistance Program." *NASSP Bulletin* 76 No. 549 (1993): 10-20.

DeJong, W. *Building the Peace: The Resolving Conflict Creatively Program*. Washington, DC: U.S. Department of Justice, 1993. (ERIC Document Reproduction Service No. ED 379 562).

Ferguson, V. "Encouragement From a High Profile Visitor," *The Hartford Courant*, 11 June 1997, Sec. B, 2 (4N).

Gibbs. "It's Only Me," *Time*, 19 March 2001, 22.

Green, Rick. "Skipping School," *The Hartford Courant*, 22 June 1997, Sec. A, 1 (4N).

Green, Rick. "Control Eludes State Teachers," *The Hartford Courant*, 7 July 2000, Sec. A, 3 (4N).

Green, Rick. "Kicking Out the Problem," *The Hartford Courant*, 6 July 2000, sec. A, 1 (4N).

Grossnickle, D., and F. Sesko. *Promoting Effective Discipline in School and Classroom: A Practitioner's Perspective*, 1985. (ISBN: 0-88210-170-6) Reston, VA: National Association of Secondary School Principals.

Heller, G.S. "Changing the School to Reduce Student Violence: What Works?" *NAASP Bulletin* (April 1996): 1-10.

Johnson, D.W., and R.T. Johnson. "Reducing School Violence through Conflict Resolution Training." *NAASP Bulletin* (April 1996): 11-18.

Kaplan, N.M. "Student Mediation: Opportunity and Challenge. *National School Safety Center News Journal* (Winter, 1996): 8-10.

Kenworthy, Tom. "A School in Agony." *The Hartford Courant,* 21 April 1999, Sec. A, 1 (4N).

Kenworthy, Tom. "Fear Took Over Schools Outside as Well as In." *The Hartford Courant,* 21 April 1999, Sec. A, 1 (4N).

Megan, Kathleen. "The Life, Times and Money of the Teenager," *The Hartford Courant,* 29 Dec. 1999, Sec. D, 1 (4N).

Moore, D., and J. Forster. "Student Assistance Program: New Approaches for Reducing Adolescent Substance Abuse. *Journal of Counseling and Development.* 71 No. 3 (1993): 326-329.

Morse, Jodie. "Girlhoods Interrupted," *Time,* 19 March 2001, 28.

National Education Goals Panel. *The National Education Goals Report Executive Summary. Improving Education Through Family-School-Community Partnerships,* 1995. (ISBN: 0-16-048364-6). Washington, DC: U.S. Printing Office: 3.

Noguerra, P.A. "Alternatives to Get-Tough Measures Can Produce Students with a Sense of Community." *The School Administrator* (Feb. 1996): 8-13.

Pagnozzi, Amy. "When Will We Do More Than Watch?" *The Hartford Courant,* 26 April 1999, Sec. A, 9 (4N).

Patteson, Jean. "Dressing Up, Dressing Down," *The Orlando Sentinel,* as published in *The Hartford Courant,* 5 July 2000, Sec. D, 3 (4N).

Prothrow-Stith, M.D., Deborah. *Violence Prevention Curriculum for Adolescents.* Newton, MA: Educational Development Center, Inc., 1987.

Reitz, Stephanie. "Dress Code Surveys Coming In." *The Hartford Courant,* 8 Feb. 2000, Sec. B, 2 (4N).

Rosemond, John. "Powerless Public Schools Cannot Prevent Tragedies." *The Hartford Courant,* 2 May 1999, Sec. H. 7 (4N).

"Schools Try Uniforms to Restore Discipline." *The Hartford Courant,* 3 March 1996, Sec. A, 12(4N).

Stansbury, Robin. "Schools Should Practice Safety Measures in Age of Danger." *The Hartford Courant,* 21 April 1999, Sec. A, 15 (4N).

Stratton, J. *How Students Have Changed. A Call to Action for Our Children's Future.* (ISBN: 0-87652-220-7). (Library of Congress Catalog Card No.: 95-078343), (AASA Stock No.: 21-00527), 1995. American Association of School Administrators: 9.

Sullivan, Robert. "What Makes a Child Resilient?" *Time,* 19 March 2001, 35.

Toch, Thomas, Ted Gest, and Monica Guttman. "Violence in Schools: When Killers Come to Class, *U.S. News & World Report,* 8 Nov. 1993, 31.

U.S. Department of Education. *Strong Families, Strong Schools,* 1994. (ISBN: 1994-381-888). Washington, DC: U.S. Government Printing Office, III.

"Violence Plagues Schools Across France." *The Hartford Courant,* 19 Feb. 2000, Sec. A, 3 (4N).

East Hartford High School
Student Assistance Center Awards

2000/2001	The Governor's Prevention Partnership— 10th Anniversary Award for Student Assistance
2000/2001	The Governor's Prevention Partnership— Outstanding Contributions to Student Assistance
1998/1999	The Hartford Courant—Tapestry Award Exceptional Programs in Diversity
1998/1999	State of Connecticut—Department of Education Challenge to Educational Citizenship Award
1996/1997	ERASE—East of the River Action for Substance Abuse Elimination Local Substance Abuse Prevention Award
1995/1996	USA Today Community Solutions for Education Award
1995/1996	State of Connecticut Governor's Youth Action Award
1995/1996	East Hartford High School PTO Outstanding Contributions to Youth Award
1995/1996	Town of East Hartford—Department of Youth Services Community Involvement Award
1994/1995	State of Connecticut—Drugs Don't Work Outstanding Peer Mediation Program Award
1994/1995	United States Department of Education Outstanding Programs for At-Risk Students Award
1993/1994	Capitol Region Education Council Achievement in Cultural Awareness Award
1993/1994	United Way (Hartford Region) Violence Reduction Award
1993/1994	CEA—Connecticut Education Association Outstanding Leadership and Service Programs Award

About the Authors

Dr. STEVEN W. EDWARDS received his bachelor of science degree from Springfield College, and a master's degree and doctorate from the University of Connecticut. A twenty-two-year veteran of the profession, he has served since 1992 as principal of East Hartford High School. Dr. Edwards has published numerous articles on the topic of student behavior and has made presentations at the state and national level on many of the innovative programs at East Hartford High School, including the development and implementation of the Student Assistance Center. Most recently, he was recognized by *The Hartford Courant* with their first Tapestry Award for promoting programs in diversity.

KENNETH J. GWOZDZ, who has been an educator for thirty years, is currently the director of the Student Assistance Center at East Hartford High School. He holds a bachelor of science degree and a master's degree. In addition to developing and implementing the Student Assistance Center, he is responsible for developing programs in the areas of alternative education, student activities, and student assistance.

MARY MEGGIE is Professional Development Coordinator for East Hartford public schools, a frontline veteran English teacher, and a Celebration of Excellence recipient recognized for innovative teaching ideas. She has also worked as a writer and reporter and holds degrees in English education, guidance counseling, and has done post-graduate work in bilingual-bicultural education. During the thirty plus years in the classroom, she has taught students of all abilities as well as students at risk. Ms. Meggie serves as a facilitator, trainer, presenter and seminar leader for the Connecticut State Department of Education's widely acclaimed Beginning Educator Support and Training (BEST) program and is active in setting educational standards as a portfolio scorer and assessor of new teachers for the state.